BABY DAYS

BABY DAYS

Activities, Ideas, and
Games for Enjoying
Daily Life with
a Child under Three

BARBARA ROWLEY

HYPERION
New York

Library of Congress Cataloging-in-Publication Data

Rowley, Barbara.
    Baby days : activities, ideas, and games for enjoying daily life with a child under three / by Barbara Rowley. —1st ed.
        p.   cm.
   ISBN 0-7868-8452-5
   1. Play.   2. Creative activities and seat work.   3. Toddlers.
4. Infants. I. Title.
HQ782.R68   2000
649'.5—dc21   99–21945
                CIP

First Edition

Designed by Nancy Singer Olaguera

10 9 8 7 6 5 4 3 2 1

For my mother
and my daughter

CONTENTS

~~~~~~~~~~~~~~~~~~~~~~~~~~~~~~~~~~~~

ACKNOWLEDGMENTS

The inspiration behind *Baby Days* is, of course, my baby Anna, now a much bigger girl, of course, and regularly reminding me of this fact as she pulls on her shoes and heads off to preschool. *Baby Days* is, in many ways, a record of my life with Anna during her first three years of life and my first three of motherhood. She continues to inspire me with her curiosity, love of fun and exploration, and constant readiness to try something new.

While Anna was my inspiration for playing, my agent Anne Depue was my inspiration for writing up these ideas. Anne encouraged me with her belief in this project professionally and, equally importantly, as a mother. In nearly every phone call we not only talked about writing and illustrations, but also the latest mother-discovery, from new ways to play with scarves to the delight of putting flour in spice jars for pretend cooking. In editor Leslie Wells at Hyperion, I found another winning combination of professional and mom; Leslie speedily moved this book along its path to being published with unwavering support, as well as the occasional conversation about the wondrous bath toy possibilities of self-sealing plastic bags. Doug Keith, the speedy illustrator who cleared the decks to do this project in a hurry, was another such combination: a dad who could really draw.

I'd also like to thank all of my magazine editors, particularly my wonderful friends at *Family Fun Magazine* who first allowed me to see that I could combine writing and fun with kids into a viable career. Alix Kennedy, Ann Hallock, Lisa Stiepock, Greg Lauzon, Jon Adolph, Deanna Cook, and Priscilla Totten have all been unfailing supporters and many of the ideas in this book have their genesis in projects I've done for *Family Fun* over the years. My editors at *Parenting Magazine* have also been terrific friends professionally and personally, and I thank editors Josh Lerman, Dan Shapiro, and Linda Rodgers for their consistent support, and the assignments that sustained me and informed this project.

Along with my editors, I also must thank the other parents of young children who generously gave me the wisdom of their own unique perspectives. Lori Langston, Lulu Lanagan, Jill Ridill, Jacquie Persons, Kim Speek, and Kim Head thoughtfully plowed through this manuscript and offered suggestions and advice, even as their own little ones pulled at their sleeves. Their input is very much in evidence in these pages. Meanwhile, my own daughter was kept happy for a few hours of writing time a day, at least, by my friends Elizabeth Severn, Lori Rauschenberg, Krista Wright, Cheryl Nymann, and Michelle McGiveny.

Finally, thanks are due to my parents and to my dear friends Teresa Riordan, Kate Nolan, Joe Crump, Jill Ridill, Kim Speek, Edeen Hill, Bar Turner, Ginger Povah, Don Hart, Jessica Kircher, Betsy Jasper, Denise Wade, Susan Flint, Molly Clark, Carlotta Avery (and everyone at Sanborn Camps), and of course, my best friend and husband, Taylor Middleton. Life, like books, doesn't always go smoothly. I couldn't have made it through the bumps of this past year without their support and encouragement.

BABY DAYS

Introduction

~~~~~~

WELCOME TO
BABY DAYS

It's true. You *will* look back on these years as some of the most special of your family's life. If you've just brought home a baby, the next three years will be full of excitement as you watch your child quickly mature from infancy through toddlerhood, mastering everything from walking to talking and possibly even starting preschool. But along with being the most enchanting, these are also surely the most exhausting of times for parents and caregivers, and often, the most challenging.

More than one parent, in a haze after a seemingly sleepless night and having already wiped down the high chair and changed two diapers and cleaned up the floor and put out the blocks and put them back, has looked at their still-ready-to-play child and suddenly realized in a state approaching despair: *It's only 9:00 in the morning. What am I going to do with her for the rest of the day?* Welcome to baby *daze*.

A sudden inability to think about what to do next is common among all parents of young children. In addition to the actual tedium of simply attending to their basic daily needs, keeping children busy whose average attention span is around 15 minutes—on a good day—is no easy task. And yet it is a task that parents and caregivers know now that they must take seriously. Study after study points to the first three years of life as a critical time in a young child's social, emotional, intellectual, and physical development. The experiences children have, or fail to have, during these years, do make a difference. For parents and other caregivers of young children, this information can pose a heavy burden. How can they think of enough activities to keep the young child in their life challenged and interested? And how can they possibly fit anything else into an already demanding schedule of feeding, cleaning, soothing, and caring for a young child?

In *Baby Days*, you'll find ways to incorporate enriching, educational, or just plain fun activities into this hectic schedule. How is this possible? Because the activities and ideas are specifically designed and selected to fit into some of the more predictable time periods in family life. These include the occasional leisurely morning when you have time or energy to try before-nap-time projects with baby, the meal times when you must cook while watching your child, the hectic late afternoon when you need to organize activities that you can supervise from a distance, as well as the car trip you'd really like to take without your little one screaming from the backseat.

Instead of having to adapt an activity to fit your situation—something that requires a little more planning and imagination than the average-in-the-thick-of-it parent can sometimes muster—in *Baby Days*, you can look up an activity to fit the situation you find yourself in. And because babies *are* babies, many of the same daily situations exist for every family. All young children have longer periods of wakefulness at certain points in the day and are sleepy or grouchy at others. They all have to be fed and bathed and diapered, and they often have to be taken out of the home either for errands or for special outings.

Caregivers, too, have predictable needs. They must sometimes take care of a young child while fixing a meal or answering the phone or running a quick errand. And they require, a lot of the time, games and projects to do with baby that capture their own imaginations. Taking care of a baby day in, day out is hard work. Adults need ways to intersperse the tedium of physically caring for the child in their care with some gratifying fun and bonding time for both of them. Bored caregivers are usually boring to baby as well as to themselves— a lose-lose situation.

Of course, babies, parents, schedules, and families are far from uniform. Yours, like every family, has its own idiosyncrasies, from the personalities and number of people in it to where you live and what you do for a living. As a result, your child's nap, eating, and bedtime schedules and your own daily routine may be different from what is described in this book. Your personality and tastes, as well as those of the child or children in your care, will also make a difference in how, when, why, and even if you choose to try some of the activities in this book.

Think of *Baby Days* as a kind of cookbook of tricks, activities, and suggestions that you will want to scrutinize for your family's particular needs. In a recipe book, if you don't like fish, you skip that section without a moment's guilt. And if you never eat eggs for breakfast but love them for dinner, you simply look up egg dishes under "Breakfast" and use the recipes later. Only you know when certain types of activities work best in your home and what your child, and yourself, will most enjoy. So don't make your child eat asparagus, and don't force yourself to introduce finger painting if you know it will drive you absolutely crazy. It's almost impossible to enjoy anything, whether it is food or fun, when you are motivated by guilt or by a feeling that something must be done for its own sake, regardless of the consequences.

By the same token, trying new things when you or your

baby is in the mood for them can teach you a lot about your own capabilities, strengths, and interests and, more importantly, about those of your child. As you probably do regularly with a recipe book, think about ways to change things to suit you and your family's tastes and peculiarities. If you can't stand the thought of getting paint everywhere, why not finger-paint outside, in swimsuits? In cooking, much of the fun is in experimenting, adapting, and trying the unexpected. The same is true with playing with your young child and using the activities in this book. Sometimes you really don't know what you like—or don't like—until you try it.

And then again, sometimes you don't have the time—or the inclination—to cook anything at all. You don't feel compelled to fix a multi-course meal every day; when you are thinking about or planning for time to spend with your baby, go easy on yourself. You don't have to spend every minute of the day engaging your child in new activities. Follow your child's lead and your own instincts: When the old games, toys, and activities are getting boring for one or both of you, add something new to the menu.

How to Use This Book

Start by looking at the chapters that describe what you are doing right now or what you will be doing soon. To make selection even faster and easier, *Baby Days* is organized in every chapter first by ages, starting with activities for the very youngest children. Then, at the top of each activity, you'll find a box that highlights the critical information you need to know before you get started: not only the age appropriateness of an activity, but suggestions on what special skills it may require, as well as the sorts of interests it may appeal to in your child.

Of course there may be times when children are ready, in terms of skill and interest, for an activity before the listed ages, and times when they are uninterested or unable to do an activity even when they exceed the recommended age. Only you can make such determinations, so keep an eye out for descriptions that fit what your child is doing right now and is interested in, regardless of his or her age.

When you are especially pressed for time, you'll find the subsequent listings in the information box—preparation time and messiness quotient—very helpful in determining what activities you can handle and when. Note, however, that preparation time only applies to how much time might be required to get ready for a project. It is nearly impossible to tell how long each activity will hold your child's interest and exactly how it will do this. Some children can spend what seems like an inordinate amount of time simply poking their fingers and making holes in a lump of play clay and never really pick it up to play with it in the ways you might have expected. Others will latch on to one item you've set out and ignore everything else. However your child safely amuses himself with the things you've provided, you can count your efforts as successful. Watching your child take an activity in a new and creative direction is indeed one of the great joys of parenthood. There is no right way to play, so if you've got the time, let each activity run its course, whatever your child determines that may be. Never interrupt a happy and interested child if you can avoid it. Instead, watch what intrigues your child and catches her interest. You'll be gaining insight into your child and forming ideas about activities you might try or invent that would be even more customized and appropriate.

A Note to Families with More Than One

Parents with more than one child can look for a listing entitled "The Sibling Factor," which appears, when relevant, above many activities. Of course, as anyone who has invited older children into their home can affirm, play is inherently adaptable. Grade school children will reach for a baby's toy and use it in a new, more sophisticated way. Toddlers and preschoolers and kindergartners can often work side-by-side on the same kind of projects. Older children, having more skills, are inclined to take play in more advanced directions, but they still like to have fun in many of the same ways as children do who may be much younger. Many of the activities in *Baby Days* can become family favorites that last well into grade school. And many will also give older children a way to play and interact with their pre-verbal little brother or sister, something most are anxious to do right away. Of course, some activities will be more difficult when there is more than one child to supervise, and you'll often need to have at least twice as many tools on hand in order to add extra players. You'll find cautionary notes relevant to such problems throughout the book.

A Few Words about Safety

Finally, be sure to read the commonsense cautions that appear with many activities. While *Baby Days* is not a safety manual, safety considerations are noted throughout. However, these safety cautions are by no means all-inclusive, and will not replace or render unnecessary the cautious caregiver's eye. The activities in *Baby Days* are designed to be used with close adult supervision, and many are not appropriate without this one-on-one attentiveness. Left to their own devices, children are amazingly inventive in the ways they can find to harm themselves. In fact, unintentional injury is the leading cause of death of children in the United States.

In particular, children can find ways to choke on small items, strangle themselves on any available hanging string or fabric, trip and fall down, eat the wrong things, drown themselves in small amounts of water, or burn themselves on hot stoves. They don't set out to hurt themselves; they are just exploring. But most of these injuries occur during unsupervised explorations. You want to keep obvious dangers such as sharp knives, poisons, hot substances, and hard and throat-size objects out of reach of a child who constantly, or even occasionally, pops things in his mouth. And you want to childproof your environment as much as possible, padding sharp corners, gating stairs, and so forth. But many of the other dangers can't be completely removed or guarded against by physical adaptations—nor should they be. Children need to splash in water, glue tiny pieces of pasta onto paper, run races, and climb. They just need an ever-attentive guide—you—in order for their ventures to be safe.

Getting Ready for Baby Days

First, of course, you must babyproof your home for safety. Walking through your home shortly after (or even before) you bring baby home, you'll want to look for and take measures to prevent the hazards of falls, choking, strangulation, fire, poisoning, electrocution, and more. These measures are detailed in many baby-care manuals.

But after you walk around and look at your home with an eye toward babyproofing it, why not take another walk (and a crawl) around and think about baby-welcoming it as well? There is much that can be done to make your home more fun and accessible to a child under three (which, in turn, makes it more fun and easier for you), and much of this takes place outside of the nursery or baby's room, the typical places parents concentrate their efforts before bringing home a new baby.

After all, aside from the time a child spends sleeping and dressing there, most children under three don't spend all that much time in their rooms. And why would they? Most of the activity in the house involving you takes place in the kitchen, the laundry room, the living room, and the bathroom. And children under three most definitely want to be where the action—and you—are. And, of course, that is where you want your child as well: right where you can keep an eye on him.

To make your house run more smoothly in the baby days

ahead, you need to think about ways to integrate your child into its central spaces, as well as think about ways to use easy-to-reach areas where you can store the day-to-day tools you and your young child will need on a regular basis.

Start with the Kitchen

There's a reason why so many parents recommend that you clean out a baby-level cupboard in your kitchen and fill it with baby-safe plastics, wooden spoons, and pans: It works, and it can keep your baby happily occupied while you try to get simple things done, like unloading the dishwasher. But one cabinet is just one cabinet—not enough to amuse your baby indefinitely in the kitchen.

Since the kitchen is where you will spend so much of your time either with baby, or while you are trying to cook, eat, clean, and so forth, it pays to think about ways to extend the playtime options in what is often the center of any home. For safety's sake, keep play areas close enough that you can monitor them, but out of the way of traffic. This is particularly important in the kitchen, where you may be carrying hot food or sharp objects as you walk from place to place. Some possibilities:

Birth to One Year

- Put a tape or CD player in a handy spot, with a basket of classical and baby music beside it.

- Hang a wind chime or a light catcher out a nearby window.

- Keep a small basket of favorite toys—rattles, balls, teething rings, and anything you may turn up in your kitchen (many babies love a set of plastic measuring cups)—in a corner or on an accessible shelf or cabinet.

❍ Set a small basket of wooden blocks out for beginning builders around one year old.

❍ Hang a child-safe mirror on the wall near where you often set your child to eat, play, or watch you, so he can watch himself at the same time.

One Year and Up

❍ If you have the room, invest in a child-size set of table and chairs for your child to eat and play at while you work in the kitchen.

❍ Purchase or make (see Chapter 3, "Nap Times") child-safe magnets (in other words, too large to ingest) for your refrigerator's door. If your door isn't metal, consider creating a magnet-holding surface by framing a piece of tin in wood (to cover sharp edges) and hanging it on a low-lying blank wall. And don't forget the possibility of magnet play on the outside of a washing machine in the laundry room. One fun homemade variation: Attach magnets to paper cups and hang them up on the refrigerator or washer. Your child can fill them with various treasures, or toss balls into them, or simply see how much the cups—and magnets— can hold before a cup tips or falls.

❍ A set of open bookshelves, if you have the space in your kitchen, laundry area, or breakfast room, can serve as your baby's special central play place for years to come. Use the low shelves to store toys, books, and blocks, sorted by category in boxes or baskets. Before long, as your child sees and helps you put these items back where they belong on a regular basis, she will begin to learn that like objects go with like objects—an important beginning of logic skills. Keep toys you want to monitor usage of in the early years, such as crayons or markers, within your own reach on higher shelves, as well as things only you need: reference books, bibs, baby wipes, and so forth. *Commonsense Caution: Be sure to bolt the shelves to the wall. Babies pulling themselves up and young climbers with an eye on the upper reaches can accidentally pull the shelves down on themselves.*

◑ Create a plastic bucket full of child-safe cleaning supplies: a spray bottle filled with water, several rags or brushes (old toothbrushes make particularly good scrubbers for tiny hands), a plastic bowl, even a whisk broom. Pull out your child's bucket out along with your own when there is cleaning to be done.

◑ Hang or set a child-size broom (push brooms are easiest for young children to use) next to your own.

◑ Paint the inside of your child's play cabinet with chalkboard paint (available at most paint stores) for a now-you-see-it, now-you-don't chalkboard. Get glow-in-the-dark chalk for him to draw with if he likes to shut himself inside, and tie a ribbon to the outside handle to let him pull the door shut by himself. *Commonsense Caution: Teach your child early about the finger-pinching effect of hinges and closing doors, and make certain he can't trap himself inside.*

Two Years and Up

◑ Consider the possibilities of low and out-from-underfoot wall space as play areas, and temporarily mount some play toys on the wall. You can easily hang a felt board or chalkboard at a low level (be aware that chalk might get on the walls, however). You can even mount things like tiny steering wheels, levers, drums, or even a xylophone to a piece of plywood and hang it out of the way where you won't stumble over it on the floor while you cook. Many young children prefer to stand and play, effectively keeping everything and everyone out of your way. When company comes, just lift the contraption off the wall and set it aside.

◐ Keep a supply of scrap or construction paper handy for your child to reach on her own, along with a few select art supplies that you know your child can handle relatively unsupervised.

◐ Devote a drawer to your assistant chef's cooking supplies: wooden spoons, mixing bowls, plastic knives, cookie cutters, spice jars, or any other tool your child regularly uses with you while you cook together. Your child will feel proud and helpful when you ask for a mixing spoon, and he can go get it.

◐ Hang a bulletin board for displaying homemade art and other items of interest to your child near or above her desk. To avoid fallen—and later, stepped on—thumbtacks, hot-glue a half-dozen or more clothespins to the board (see description of low-temperature hot-glue gun under "Get Organized and Prepared" section later in the chapter). You and your child can use these to safely hang items of interest.

◐ Start a toddler recycling basket where you can toss all sorts of unneeded odds and ends—the juice lid, the weird box—that, for whatever reason, you just know your child would love. Pull this basket of free toys out whenever you need a quick project to keep your child occupied.

Then, Consider the Rest of Your House

There are many other ways to integrate your child's needs and desires into your home beyond the kitchen, all of which will ultimately help you keep the house more organized, make getting things done easier, and keep everyone happier. If your child doesn't have to carry toys with him everywhere he goes,

you won't have to run around putting them back quite so often.

Scale Things Down

First, think about ways you can scale things down to make life
easier for your resident short person. You won't have to ask her
to hang up her coat quite so often if you install coat hangers
at her level. And she won't have to beg you desperately for a
snack if you keep a few low-mess snacks like fruit roll-ups or
granola bars in a basket in just her reach. As your baby becomes
a toddler, finding ways to solve the issues that are making her
ask you to do things constantly—or vice versa—will make both
of your lives easier and happier and will help your child develop independence and self-sufficiency. For instance, you
may find that letting your child use the bathtub as a sink will
safeguard your back: She can stand and wash her hands or even
brush her teeth at the faucet. And several well-placed stools
throughout the house will save you from numerous lift-me-
ups. (Do monitor their use, however, and make sure they are
sturdy and steady. Many tiny stools can tip easily when used
incorrectly.)

Think about Toys and Toy Storage

No doubt your home is forever overrun with toys. Friends
and family are generous, and the lure of a new toy might be
hard for you to resist as well. After all, toys for very young
children are in many ways more about you than them, for they
are what you buy in the hopes that you are purchasing your
child a few moments of engaging solo play (and yourself a potential break) or providing yourself something new to do with
baby.

Your young child—who probably can't even talk to express
his desires—won't be spoiled by things he never asked for. He

might, however, be overwhelmed by them or simply fail to find them when you want him to, particularly if they are all tossed together in a closed box. For many young children, pulling everything out of the box can become the activity. Once everything is dumped out, the game is over.

Squeezing time in your daily schedule to keep toys organized and accessible on open shelves, arranged by category in baskets or open boxes and set about throughout the house where baby can find them and play with them on the spot, can be helpful to you both. For instance, you might think about putting blocks in a box near a flat surface for easy stacking, balls in a basket in the laundry room if this is where you like to play Catch and Roll, tiny dishes and tea sets on a low shelf in the kitchen, and an assortment of puzzles, shape sorters, books, and bead coasters in your own room, where your child can play quietly with them as you wake up.

From the start, keeping things sorted by categories and in places that make sense for play will help your child gain an early understanding of order and logic and ultimately help her become more self-sufficient. She will know where to look for things and where to put them back. And so will you.

Look For and Create Special Hide-Aways

In a world that is most definitely out-sized for them, it is comforting for children to find spaces and areas that are small and cozy and devoted just to them. Sometimes these spaces can be found in surprising places. A finished, medium-to-large closet with a light inside and emptied of everything but your child's toys and books can become a favorite playroom. (Tape the latch on the side of the door so that it can be opened or closed with just a push, protecting your child from getting trapped in his playroom closet.) A corner of your laundry room, next to a sink if possible, might make the perfect place for setting up a permanent art studio. Toss some pillows and some favorite books and puzzles in the space behind the couch in the living room for a quiet games area. And at some point, you will appreciate your own fore-sight if you have thought to store a basket of books, toys, or blocks in every bathroom in the house.

A reading nook, for some particularly tough nap and bed-time fighters, is another hide-away worth considering. This can act as a transitional place before sleep, offering the possibility of a compromise your child can agree to—after all, it isn't ac-tually bed. (Of course, for another child, it might offer simply another way to delay the inevitable, if he refuses to go from there to the bed or crib. If you choose to set up a reading nook, you'll quickly see which way it will work for you and your child.)

To set up a reading nook, look for a cozy corner of your child's room (or some other out-of-the-way room in your house) where you can create a permanent nest of pillows, blan-kets, and stuffed animals, and even drape a sheet or blanket over a rod or suspend one from the ceiling, to make it especially dark and private. You'll also need a lamp to read by, of course, and a tape player with soft music on it. And if the corner can be next to a bookshelf, so much the better.

Think about a theme while you make your hide-away: Are you creating a little cave, a corner in the forest, or a secret spot in the sea? You can decorate accordingly. If you can make your reading corner a permanent place, dark green or black chalk paint (which turns surfaces into chalkboards and is available at most paint stores) can be applied to the wall to form bushes, trees or a forest, or a cave—and a writing surface during story time. Glow-in-the-dark stickers stuck to the walls and ceiling to lightly illuminate the space are also a nice touch; they come in celestial and sea creature shapes. You might also consider hanging a felt board (see Chapter 3, "Nap Times," for directions on making one). Felt sets of the char-acters in many of your child's favorite stories are widely avail-

able, allowing you the option of a pre-bedtime felt-board "puppet" show.

The key is to make your space cozy, comfortable, and relatively small—kids love to snuggle in such spaces, especially with their parents beside them. Simply being in this space, if it is set up correctly, will quiet your child down. And it doesn't necessarily have to be used only at bedtime. Anytime you need a quiet, settled atmosphere, simply suggest a few books in the nook. When it is a matter of curling up with Mom or Dad in a small place with a good book, this option is usually irresistible.

Get Organized and Prepared for Crafts and Projects

With children under three, you can't plan craft events, you must do them when the time arises—whenever that happens. This means that if you aren't prepared, you won't do crafts. Set aside an afternoon to shop and then outfit your craft cupboard with all the supplies you'll need over the next few years, and you'll always be able to pull off an activity at a moment's notice. Shop for the supplies below as suggested, then organize them in a handy but out-of-baby's-reach cabinet during your child's afternoon nap. As your child gets older, you might change this location, moving at least those supplies you want your child to be able to get down on his or her own.

Plastic buckets or open plastic totes with handles work especially well for holding craft items, particularly if you use them to corral and categorize supplies. If you put all the paints and drawing items in one container, for example, all the cutting and pasting items in another, and all the molding and homemade play-clay ingredients supplies in another, you can easily grab the one you need and carry it to your child's work space, and just as easily throw everything back and return it to the cupboard when you have finished.

Supplies from the Craft or School Supply Store

Washable Paints: Buy paint colors in individual spill-proof containers.

Paintbrushes: Since babies have a difficult time washing brushes when they change paint colors, buy enough brushes so that you can put a different brush in each paint container. And for a change of pace or for use as throw-away paintbrushes when you travel, put a supply of cotton-tipped ear swabs or toothpicks with your crafts to use as impromptu brushes.

Tempera Paints: Buy a selection of both dry and pre-mixed paints, making sure both are washable.

Washable Markers: An incredible variety of specialty markers are available. For now, just buy the plain versions; fancier types, like color changers or stamp markers, aren't worth it for most children under three, who won't appreciate the effects or be able to manipulate the stamps effectively. As you set out the markers, make a point of getting rid of or removing from general use all your non-washable markers. If you don't, they'll surely find a way to mix with the washable variety— and to adorn your walls. If and when your markers dry out when they are left without their caps, dip the ends in hot water for 2 minutes to revive them.

Crayons: Since the advent of markers, crayons aren't essential for kids under two, who have to press too hard with crayons to make a satisfactory color and so often prefer markers. But two-year-olds and up love crayons. Keep several packs around for use at home and on the road, stored in plastic containers with tops. You won't be able to keep them all lined up in their cardboard box (which usually starts falling apart) for long, so store them as suggested here to save yourself some time and energy later on.

Chalk, Chalkboard Eraser, and Chalkboard and Washable, No-Alcohol Dry-Erase Markers and a Dry-Erase Board: Being able to draw—and erase one's drawing—is a special kind of magic for children over two years of age. Washable, alcohol-free (and thus, not so smelly) versions of dry-erase markers provide high-tech erasable technology that is especially fun. Consider getting travel-size chalk and dry-erase boards for use in the car.

Washable Glue: The easiest kind of glue for young children to use is a glue stick, but for bigger projects that require gluing heavier objects, you'll want white glue, which is also an ingredient in other craft recipes. Pour it into tiny cups or onto paper plates, and to control the mess let your child access it with an ear swab. Glitter glue is also a wonderful innovation for the pre-three-year-old, which eliminates the messiness of loose glitter (and the potential hazard of its getting in a child's eye).

Tape: Masking tape (look for the colored varieties, if possible), clear tape, and double-sided tape should be craft-closet staples.

Paper: Keep scrap paper and a package of construction paper handy for casual drawing and painting sessions. A roll of butcher-block paper—about $25—is also great for covering work surfaces, painting large murals, making wrapping paper, and playing games. You can get a wall-mounting holder for the huge roll through butcher supply stores (check the Internet) for an additional $25. The whole set up will probably last your family through grade school. Finally, get several packages of blank greeting cards and envelopes. Pull them out for your child to paint on or to draw personalized thank-you notes and birthday cards. You can make your own cards, of course, by folding over a piece of paper, but how do you send them in the mail? Blank cards solve that problem.

Scissors: Children under three usually have a hard time using scissors. Some craft companies (such as NASCO, 800-962-7269) make trainer scissors that allow you to handle the scissors at the same time your child does or that have a spring that lets your child just pinch the scissors open and shut, with no pulling motion necessary. If your toddler is showing interest in cutting, consider getting a pair.

Smock: An old T-shirt, a pillowcase with arm and head holes cut in the corners and top, or a store-bought art smock will work for helping keep your child clean. Or, if it is warm enough, strip him down to diapers during messy craft sessions and plan an after-activity bath.

Small Stuff: A selection of beads, feathers, pipe cleaners, clothespins, and wooden spools will always serve you well, as will a few Styrofoam forms in cone, square, and egg shapes.

(Low-Temperature) Hot-Glue Gun: You don't want your child anywhere near a hot-glue gun, but keeping one on hand for you to use will make you a superhero in your child's eyes when doing crafts and all sorts of fix-its around the home. Even a low-temperature glue gun (which is somewhat safer for you to use, and readily available) will allow you to quickly repair crafts, glue the seemingly ungluable, and mend all sorts of broken treasures. Get one and keep it locked up and out of reach.

Supplies from the Grocery

Even if you keep the following supplies in your kitchen already, get extra to keep with your craft supplies. You'll only have to go to one place to find things, and you won't accidentally eat up your supplies during dinner.

Food Coloring: You'll need a selection of different colors for dyeing food and homemade clays, glues and paints, lotions and snow. The pastes—available in the cake-decorating section of some groceries and in craft stores—work best, but the drops are fine too.

Cookie Cutters: You'll use them for shaping clay and cutting stencils, and in making cookies and sandwiches. A large supply of cookie cutters will always be useful in your home, whether you eat sweets or not.

Shaped Pasta, Colored Beans: These inexpensive culinary items will form the basis of many crafts and games. Best bets: pasta you can string—like macaroni and penne—and various colors of beans, like those in bags labeled for seven-bean soup. Buy a bag or two for the crafts cupboard and you'll be stocked for a long time to come. To color your pasta, simply mix a dab of food coloring with a tablespoon of rubbing alcohol and pour the mixture over the pasta on a cookie sheet, mixing it until the pasta is evenly coated.

Corn Starch, Cream of Tartar, Alum, Salt, Baking Soda, Flour: All of these items are called for again and again in different dough and craft recipes. Keep a supply separate from your baking area so you'll never run unexpectedly short while baking or doing crafts.

Wax Paper: This is the best surface for finger painting.

Liquid Starch, Borax, White Soap Flakes, Dawn Dishwashing Soap: Look in the detergent section for these handy ingredients, used in finger paints, flower drying, and dough creations, as well as for ultimate homemade bubbles.

Toothpicks: Buy the flat kind with a rounded tip. You'll use them for any number of sculptures. Plus, two-year-olds love to skewer their food with them (you'll want to monitor this activity, though).

Glycerin: For making long-lasting bubbles, this is the key ingredient. You'll find it in the pharmacy section.

A Few Words about the Television Temptation

Many legitimate things keep us from doing the things we want to do with our young children. We work. We need time for ourselves. We have to sleep, don't we? But one thing that keeps us from interacting with our children is clearly within our control. Actually, our remote control. It's the television. It's not a crime to plop your child in front of the tube, but it's nothing to pat yourself on the back for either, no matter what kind of educational programming they are watching. Even—or maybe especially—with children under three, it's very important to think about the precedents you are setting when you introduce television to your child as part of their regular routine. It's worth noting that the American Academy of Pediatrics recommends *no* television for children under two.

Nevertheless, television (and this includes videos) is an easy crutch that we all sometimes feel the need to use. But if you turn the television on when you don't have time to think up something better for your child to do, you'll be teaching your child to do the same thing. Most parents want to raise a self-entertaining child, who doesn't just go for the television as an activity before coming up with something more creative. As hard as it is, and it can be plenty hard when you are in the thick of it or when you have your own television habit to deal with, try to think up something else to entertain your child and you'll save yourself from future television battles years down the road after your child has learned too well the lesson about television you've inadvertently taught him—to watch it.

Instead, consider teaching your child, and possibly yourself as well, a different television life lesson: how to use television in the healthiest, smartest ways.

Practice and teach planned television and video watching. Few parents want their children to grow up to be television monsters. They want them to read, play independently, get exercise, have hobbies. So parents must model these behaviors from the beginning. They should also practice and teach planned television watching. Turn the television on yourself only when you have a specific show you want to watch, and then turn it off. Better yet, don't watch television at all unless your child is asleep or out of the house. Because if she's awake, you've definitely got better things to do.

Move the television into a less central part of the house, so that collective viewing is more difficult. This strategy alone will cut down on most of your child's viewing, as young children want to be with their parents. And if you can't do something else—like cook dinner—while you watch, you'll cut your own viewing down as well. So what do you do while you cook, instead? See Chapter 2, "Meal Times," for ideas that are far more interactive and educational than any programming you can find. Or, if you don't want your child or children underfoot in the kitchen, look for activities that are quick and easy to supervise while you do something else; these are found in Chapter 4, "Afternoons." As for entertaining yourself? Remember the possibilities of radio, music, and even books on tape when you need a while-you-get-things-done diversion. With these options, unlike with television, you can listen while you watch your child or play with him, cook your dinner, or do your laundry.

Be aware of what—and how much—television your child is watching. Teach your child how to watch a single program and then turn it off and move on to something else. In addition to being simply a good way to learn to watch television, one that enhances both program choice and quality of viewing, this limitation of your child's viewing will help you monitor how much time she is spending daily in front of the tube.

Use television for specific purposes. Because television uses so little of the brain, it can be soothing to an over-tired or ill child. Use television when you don't want your child stimulated, when he is cranky after a nap or ill, for example. Movie nights, complete with snacks and pillows and a really good show and lots of cuddling, truly do offer fine family fun every once in a while. But make these nights special, the exception rather than the rule. And center them around one good video that you've rented or a program you know is on and plan to watch.

Understand the educational limits of television. Television is not a whole-brain activity. Not even educational television. The problem with all television is that while your child watches, he is not moving, talking, exploring, feeling, or using his senses. Most of his brain, then, is inactive. Of course, the material in educational or family-oriented television and movies is much better than the rest, but it is even further improved if you watch along and expand on what is happening conversationally. And television programs that require children to respond to what is on the screen are also better than those activities that encourage passivity. Play exercise, dance, or language videos and follow along with your child, and you'll neutralize at least some of the negatives of television watching.

Cut out the commercial. When possible, show your child only videos or commercial-free public television. On regular channels the programs may be fine, but they are often interrupted by commercials that are not. Television introduces your child to the world of the commercial and the hard-sell. How early do you want your child to be asking for the latest trendy toy or movie?

Treasure your family time. Television is a time user. Television takes away time that families could spend learning, talking, and being together. In most busy lives, there is not enough of this time, let alone time to waste it. And if you consider that your toddler spends up to half of his day sleeping, how many of his waking hours are there left to squander in this way?

Chapter One

~~~~~~~~~~

MORNINGS

Projects and Activities for Quality and Quantity Times

Morning is the ideal time to try activities that require more attention from your child and more preparation on your part. You may (depending on your baby's sleep schedule the night before) have more energy for cleanup, and your child will probably have more patience to wait for you to get organized. And whether you are a night owl who always finds mornings difficult or just a compulsive pre-planner, you can use the night before to get set for the following morning. This is a particularly good idea if your baby is waking you at night but not sleeping later in the morning. On days like these, you'll be glad to have some activities all ready to go. For all of these reasons, a morning at home can be a perfect time for messy projects like arts and crafts and other hands-on explorations.

Of course, attempting any kind of project-like play with children under three is full of potential challenges. They will make a mess. They will waste things. They might be finished before you feel you've gotten started. And in the end, they may not even care about what they've made or done. Nevertheless, all of these things are exactly what make undertaking art and other messy hands-on projects at home so important.

The fact is, messes are magical. They are the byproduct of learning and exploring, an expression of creativity and curiosity. They are also memorable breaks from a home routine that, for little kids, is often too dominated by the rather constant litany of parental control: *No, don't touch, don't spill, be careful.*

Of course, accepting mess making doesn't mean completely giving in to it. There are plenty of ways to keep mess down to a minimum without restricting creativity.

1. Keep a damp sponge in a bowl nearby for quick finger wipes while your child works.

2. Contain tiny rolling objects—like beads, rice, and so forth—by using high-sided cookie trays.

3. Cover your work surface quickly and efficiently with large old beach towels. Unlike with newspaper, there are no cracks for the mess to seep through, and you and your child can both wipe your hands dry easily on the towel while you work. When you have finished, fold up the towel and shake it out outside or throw it in the wash.

4. Throw away your mess: Save multi-sectioned containers like egg cartons or segmented cracker- or candy-box inserts to use as glue or paint palettes. Distribute small amounts of glue, paint, or small stickable objects in each section. When you have finished, just toss the whole thing in the trash.

5. Throw away your supplies: Instead of using paintbrushes, which need to be washed, substitute ear swabs, old toothbrushes, toothpicks, craft sticks, or even twigs.

6. Always consider the possibility of working outside or in a garage, where you can hose things, including your child, if necessary, down.

7. Plan messy activities before a scheduled bath or swim.

As for what ultimate product results from all this potential mayhem: Who cares? Your child won't, and neither should you. She will often enjoy the painting, pasting, building, and molding more than the final result. So put up her work on the refrigerator if you want, but if she ignores your attention and praise, don't count the experience as a waste. Enjoy the fact that your child likes art or experimentation for its own sake.

Because young attention spans are still quite short, your child may speed through the first project you've set out about the time you are relaxing into it. For this reason, and because you'll have a mess to clean up anyway with even one activity, it makes sense to always have a couple of projects ready to go. Have the needed materials out for the next activity while you are working with your child on the first, so you'll be ready to switch gears at the same time as your child, without interrupting her momentum.

You can also think about what parts of a project your child will most enjoy or which you want him to try, and do some of the initial steps yourself so he can concentrate on what he likes most. Some kids, for instance, love mixing the cookie dough but then can't keep their attention focused when the rolling and stamping part comes around. If you want him to fully experience the cutting and rolling, you might mix up the dough yourself beforehand or divide the activity into two distinct parts with time in between.

It's also helpful to organize a craft supply area (see the Introduction for a list of the items you'll need for the projects in this book) and keep it well stocked. As any parent of a pre-three-year-old knows, by the time you make it to the store and back with baby to get what you need for a potential project, it's usually time for bed, bath, or dinner—or all three.

Exercise is another great morning choice for both you and your child. It makes afternoon naps easier (for both of you, if you wish) and lunchtime appetites heartier. It also builds co-ordination and large-muscle strength and burns off energy, making everyone feel better. In addition to planning walks and outings (see Chapter 6, "Outings," for activity ideas for these events) think about turning exercise into play—such as dancing—and work into fun exercise—such as "racing" the laundry to the basket—as you go about your morning routine.

Of course, in many families, morning schedules may not often allow for long hands-on projects or even exercise on a regular basis. For these families, most mornings are a time to get the house up and running. Rather than relying on some outside, non-interactive entertainment (like television) while you do what you need to do, you can often integrate play with your child into your morning routine in many ways.

Chores with a Baby from Birth to Six Months

If you have a young baby in the house, you can move him around in his infant seat so he can get a front-row view of you at work, being careful not to put him on counters or tables where he could scoot the seat off the edge and fall. Or, for added convenience, let him happily ride around with you in a front carrier with his head facing out (if his head is strong enough to make this possible). Even if he can't face out yet, he'll enjoy accompanying you on your daily rounds and catching glimpses, sounds, and smells of what you do. Wearing your baby has the added advantage for you both of keeping you always within each other's sight and touch.

In addition to watching you, let your baby hear you as well. Chores are a great time to practice the one-sided conversation that is so helpful to baby's language development, because you have an obvious topic: Just narrate exactly what you are doing. Let baby watch you load the dishwasher and hear you name various items you put in; or remove the clothes from the dryer and toss her a warm sock to feel; or while folding the laundry, call out clothing items and colors. Put socks on your hands for baby to look at and feel—or a sock on one of baby's hands— she'll love looking at and feeling it. A baby is also a happy recipient of a shirt or sock gently tossed onto her chest or over her eyes—a great way to start a peek-a-boo game. Or let her sit there as you toss her items with different textures—nubby washcloths, silky slips, fuzzy sweaters, and so forth. If your baby's sitting up, set her in the laundry basket and give her a ride around the kitchen. If your washer or dryer has a window to the inside, let your baby sit in her seat and watch the clothes go round and round. And at the start of day be sure to let your baby watch you brush your teeth and hair and get dressed and exercise. When you talk on the phone, make a habit of looking expressively at your baby while you speak into the receiver. She'll be hearing language and feeling as though she's included in the conversation.

Chores with Crawling Babies and Walking Toddlers

For parents with older babies, chores can become more burdensome. You can try the methods described next to incorporate babies old enough to be crawling or walking about by themselves. And with children around the age of three, always look for opportunities to turn everything you do into a game, whether or not this is a race up the stairs, a challenge to toss socks in a basket, or a roving game of Hunt the Tiny Teddy Bear: While you straighten up the house, you tuck away the teddy for your child to find, and then she does the same for you. It's easy to convince your child you are actively looking for the hidden bear as you lift up and fold blankets and pick up and stack magazines.

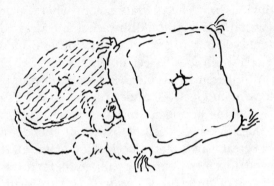

Babykeeping while Housekeeping

Using the Home Office

Once your child is walking around, it's time to outfit him with his own small chair and table, to set next to your desk and chair. In fact, this setup of home office equipment should really be a tax deduction for parents: After all, nothing will better allow you to get a few basic things done at your desk.

Give your child her own supplies as well: An old keyboard (ask around, or pick up one from a computer supply or thrift store), crayons, paper, envelopes, and an unplugged phone are essential for your young office assistant. As you work, you can give her pieces of paper to throw in the trash (a wonderful honor for many assistants), toss junk mail over for her to "read," or offer her stickers or stamps to play with. And a clear-tape dispenser can keep a near-three-year-old busy for what seems like hours, taping things together and to the desk. If she can't pull the tape off herself or you are worried about her cutting herself as well as the tape while she works, pull off a dozen little strips and place them around for her to use, or give her masking tape she can tear on her own.

You'll also want to keep old calendars, phone books, and files for your child's use: He'll treat them like treasures and probably draw all over them. Of course, you'll need to work fast while he works. At around 18 months, you'll be lucky if he works for 15 minutes, though by three, he might have edged up to half-hour intervals of drawing and pretend play. Do think twice before introducing him to any of your "real" equipment. Toddlers and computers, answering machines, or faxes can be an astoundingly bad mix for both the machinery and your nerves. There's really no reason to believe that not starting on a keyboard at two years of age will impede your child's computer literacy: By the time your child is in school, computer technology will have changed significantly. And whatever the software, most children prefer human—especially parent—instructors at this age.

Doing the Laundry

If you have an empty tissue box handy, stuff some kitchen towels inside and let your baby have fun pulling them out one by one while you get the laundry folded. And don't forget the fun of sticking your hand in a sock to turn it into a talking puppet for your baby or toddler.

You can also let your toddler help you move the laundry from washer to dryer, and have your near-three-year-old help you sort clothing into color piles and even learn to fold washcloths and dishcloths. Playing Toss or Parachute with warm sheets can also provide many fun moments, especially if you let the parachute cover both of you for a minute or two of snuggling. If your laundry room is adjacent to your kitchen, you might even give him the job of putting the dishcloths away in a reachable kitchen drawer. And keeping magnets on your washer also offers a convenient distraction while you finish up.

Washing the Dishes

Crawling babies will be drawn to the dishwasher, which isn't actually a great thing, since there are often sharp objects inside. So remove knives and other dangerous implements immediately after you open the machine, as well as any breakable glassware, and tell your child why you are doing this so she will begin to understand these hazards. Then let your child have the job of putting away the plastic containers or any other dishes you know she can safely handle. Try to load these dishes on the bottom rack, and keep them in a low, unlocked drawer or cupboard for your shorter helper's convenience.

Toddlers are usually responsible enough to hand you unbreakable items for you to put away. They will also delight in the opportunity to wash dishes themselves. Just put rubber wash and rinse tubs on a towel on the floor and let your child wash the almost-clean and unbreakable dishes by hand. You will probably have to re-wash them, but that's not the point.

Cleaning the Floors

Let your toddler help you clean cabinet doors and spotted floors with a spray bottle filled with water and a sponge. At first you'll have to constantly re-emphasize that she must wait for you to wipe up after she sprays, but soon you'll have trained a little inspector, always on the lookout for spills and spots to clean up. Eventually, she may even want to take a turn at the wiping job, besides the spraying.

Sweeping Up

As soon as your baby can walk, he'll thrill in the ability to hold the dustpan for you while you sweep. And although you'll have to monitor his progress to the trashcan (or move it closer to lower the odds of his spilling dirt on the way), he'll love dumping the dirt in the can and coming back for more. Toddlers also love to help sweep, however dubious their contribution may be, so get yours a broom of his own. Then put a masking-tape circle on the floor (far away from the part of the room where you are sweeping, if possible) and have him sweep whatever he collects with his broom into the circle. This will keep the mess partly contained, though you will have to pick up your child's dirt pile with your own broom and dustpan later. If you have floors that require vacuuming (and the sound doesn't scare your child), consider purchasing a child-size vacuum for your child or letting him carry and use one of the attachments to your adult version.

Making the Bed

Pretend to make the bed with your baby inside. Small children love this exciting version of Peek-a-boo. If you are stripping sheets, give your baby (who should be steadily sitting up) a gentle ride on the tail end of a blanket as you pull it across the floor. Changing the sheets is particularly thrilling for toddlers if you promise them the dirty ones for a bit of fort building before the sheets go into the wash. Drape them over the furniture or a pile of pillows stacked up high, or simply pull a sheet over yourselves and tuck in the ends and sit on them. Two- and three-year-olds will also enjoy using a folded sheet as a kind of trampoline for a ball or teddy bear. Put the toy in the center as you and your child hold each end tightly. Using the sheet, toss the toy into the air and catch it or watch it roll around as you lift first one side and then the other.

Outside Projects

From helping fill the bird feeders to running in the sprinklers, toddlers are wonderful yard workers. Of course, if your yard isn't enclosed (and really, even if it is), you'll need to plan only projects that enable you to watch your kids at the same time that you work. You'll find this easier if you incorporate the projects into your chores: Watering the plants or the yard or washing the driveway or sidewalks has natural appeal, but so does anything that involves picking up and bagging. You'll find toddlers enthusiastic participants in collecting sticks and leaves or picking up out-of-place pebbles.

Litter, of course, is a constant obsession among little helpers, and problematic for germ- and safety-conscious parents. Tiny gloves and a stick to poke things with, the understanding that you must make the call about what gets collected (picking up a just-discarded candy box really poses no danger), and washing their hands regularly, can all help deal with the cleanliness issue, as can understanding that the lessons being learned are good ones. You do want to teach your children that littering is bad behavior and that cleaning up is good, as long as they can do it safely and they ask you first. Most children quickly learn that they can't pick up old gum or soggy tissues, but they do of course need to be watched constantly.

In outdoor work—as in so many chores—giving children child-size tools that really work is always a great idea. Consider purchasing them a scaled-down rake, shovel, wheelbarrow, or wagon. And when they tire of outdoor work, give them activities that let them play alongside you. While you clean the garage, let them make chalk drawings on the cement; while you wash the car, let them dance barefoot in the puddles (or hold the hose, if you are really brave and prepared to get wet) or help you sponge clean the tires.

Caretaking

Set an early example of responsibility for young children by enlisting their help in taking care of pets, wild birds, and household plants. Although they are certainly not responsible enough to take on any of these projects by themselves (even a goldfish will experience feast and famine if left to their unsupervised care), they can help. Watering plants is an easy way for a just-walking toddler to participate; even a baby can be lifted to pour a small plastic glass of water into a pot. Your child can also help feed and water indoor and outdoor pets. Older toddlers will love participating in any ecological caretaking in your home, from helping to smash aluminum cans and stomp cardboard to delivering kitchen waste to the compost bin.

Commonsense Cautions for All Baby-Assisted Chores

Introducing your baby into your domestic routine will call for some alterations in your cleaning routine. Do not use spray cleansers or other toxic cleaning substances (like toilet cleansers) around the air your young child is breathing or let her have access to any cleaning solutions except soap and water. You'll also want to exercise constant supervision when your child is near household appliances of any kind. When you are working outside, your proximity to cars is a natural worry, but there are also other special considerations. In the garage, be sure to put all poisonous substances, like fertilizer, weed killer, or paint remover, well out of reach, and supervise your child closely when you are there. In the garden, teaching a very young child to pull weeds or dig can set a different kind of troublesome precedent. Make sure they are old enough to differentiate between weeds and flowers first—or you'll find your garden uprooted on the lawn. You'll also want to provide her with a designated digging area—like a sandbox—for this potentially destructive activity.

WHAT TO DO THIS MORNING

LISTEN TO MUSIC

Get into the habit of listening.

Suggested Ages: Birth and up

Your Child's Special Skills and Interests: None

Preparation Time: None

Messiness Quotient: Non-existent

The Sibling Factor: Encourage your older child to dance with you, conveniently positioned right in front of baby.

Materials: Radio, tape or CD player; portable players are especially handy if you spend a lot of time outside.

Why to try it: Child development experts and researchers say that listening to classical music (especially Mozart, in some studies) can positively impact future mathematical skills and can dramatically increase, by up to 46 percent, a child's spatial intelligence—essential for later success in calculus and physics. Common sense would indicate that classical or kids' music playing in the background while you play with your children is calming, entertaining, and even educational. Vocabularies jump as kids memorize the words to "Twinkle, Twinkle Little Star" and other songs. Listening to music also helps a child develop the ability to control impulses and learn to listen.

How to do it: While your child paints, experiments, plays with toys, or sits in a swing in the morning, make a habit of turning on a musical tape or radio station in the background. If you play a musical instrument—the piano, the guitar—get back into the habit of daily morning practice for both your and your child's sake. Later in the day, as phones ring and major appliances hum away, it is often too hectic and busy to have music playing. Classical music has been especially credited with increasing math aptitudes, and it seems particularly soothing for infants. But there may be no need to invest in a classical music library if it isn't your style: Public radio stations nationwide feature classical music, sometimes in the morning. If this isn't the case where you live, ask your local music store to recommend a few selections. Around the age of one or so, supplement this music with the classic songs of early childhood; toddlers enjoy simple tunes and lyrics that they can learn and sing along with. For a good source for children's tapes for very young children, call Music for Little People (800-346-4445). Choose tapes with the simplest songs, especially those that allow for accompanying hand motions, such as "If You Are Happy and You Know It," or "The Wheels on the Bus." The tunes may annoy you, but they have been called brilliant neurological exercises by experts such as Dr. Dee Joy Coulter, a nationally recognized neuroscience educator, who believes that they also introduce children to speech patterns, sensory motor skills, and vital movement strategies.

Possible Variations: If you have a number of young guests, organize a dance party to your child's music, even if it isn't ordinarily the kind of music you dance to. Be sure to supply scarves to wave through the air as they move. Give your sitting baby (or babies) makeshift instruments to play along—tightly sealed plastic jars filled with beans to shake, wooden-spoon drumsticks to bang—even a harmonica. With two- or three-year-olds, you can also play a variation of musical chairs: Tell them you are going to turn the music on and off, and they will have to stop moving each time the music ends. It's an exercise in self-control and surprise that toddlers (alone or in groups) find absolutely hilarious.

PLAY IN THE SUN

Give your baby diaperless time to enjoy the sun.

Suggested Ages: Birth to six months

Your Child's Special Skills and Interests: Not crawling

Preparation Time: 5 minutes

Messiness Quotient: Medium—you will have to do a load of wash.

Materials: Waterproof pads or washable sheepskins, washcloth

> **Commonsense Caution:** If you do this outside, be sure to keep exposure brief (under 10 minutes) and off-peak—before ten and after three o'clock, since sunscreen isn't recommended for babies under six months.

Why to try it: Give your baby the sensation of skin on skin, sun on skin, and freedom from the diaper.

How to do it: Strip your baby down and put him on a sheepskin or a waterproof pad covered with a soft washable blanket set near a sunny window. If the sun bothers his eyes, move his head just out of the light. Give him a few rattles and other toys. Now let him enjoy rolling around on the sheepskin, free from clothes. Keep a washcloth handy for accidents. Simply toss the materials into the washer when you are done.

SMELL, SEE, HEAR, AND TOUCH

Take your baby on a magical sensory tour.

Suggested Ages: Birth to nine months and up

Your Child's Special Skills and Interests: None

Preparation Time: None

Messiness Quotient: None

Materials: None

Why to try it: Stimulating the senses helps baby brains grow, plus it gives you something to talk about—which is handy when conversations are still one-sided.

How to do it: Put your baby in a front carrier or hold him in your arms and take him on a sensory exploration of his world. Sniff candles and baking flavor extracts. Smell the grass and the food in the refrigerator. Feel fruit in the kitchen, warm clothes in the dryer, and the sandpaper in the garage. Listen to the kitchen timer ding, and ring your own doorbell. Look carefully at the houseplants and the carpet and the patterns in the wallpaper. And as you take this walking tour of your baby's magical home, be sure to be a talkative tour guide, telling him just what it is he's seeing, smelling, hearing, and touching. When baby has had too much of all this wonderful stimulation, he'll let you know by crying or a sudden change in interest. Just resume your tour another day.

MAKE SOME SHADOWS

You exercise, your baby watches your shadow.

Suggested Ages: Birth to nine months

Your child's Special Skills and Interests: None

Preparation Time: None

Messiness Quotient: None

The Sibling Factor: A more energetic (than you) older sibling is often a willing stand-in for you in this activity. With your encouragement, he will also love making different animal and letter shadows with his body.

Materials: Bright light or sunny window

Why to try it: To a newborn, an exercising parent is much more exciting than any mobile.

How to do it: If it is at all dark outside (think December mornings) direct a light at yourself while you reach and jump, and turn your baby in her infant seat toward you and the wild shadows you are making on the wall.

Older-Child Variations: Once baby can dance herself, try the same exercises and let her make her own shadows beside you. You can also let her try to hide her shadow behind yours while you move, or take turns touching different parts of each other's shadows with funny directions, like "Put your foot in mommy's hand" or "Sit on mommy's tummy."

TICKLE 'EM PINK

Pretend face painting for babies.

Suggested Ages: Six months to one year

Preparation Time: None

Messiness Quotient: None

Your Child's Special Skills and Interests: None

The Sibling Factor: See Older-Child Variations below
for ideas.

Materials: Soft watercolor brush

Why to try it: This silly way to play with your baby is sure to capture a baby's interest and a parent's imagination.

How to do it: Using a clean, dry, soft-bristled watercolor brush, lightly touch your baby's nose and cheeks, toes and fingers, belly and head. As you touch here and there, tell baby you are painting her nose pink, her toes blue, and so forth. Make swirls and dots, lines, and designs. Tell your baby what you are doing, and giggle along with her as you tickle her pink, blue, and yellow. If baby likes the dry brush, try a slightly damp brush as well to see her reaction.

Older-Child Variations: Toddlers will also enjoy this game, though for a different reason. They'll love imagining the colors you are painting and will probably want to "paint" you too. By about the age of three, they may even want to close their eyes and guess the shape or letter you are "painting" on them, though they'll probably only be able to accurately tell the simplest shapes by touch, like squares and circles.

PLAY WITH BOXES

Stacking toys you don't have to buy.

Suggested Ages: Six months to two years

Your Child's Special Skills and Interests:
Sitting on own, stacking

Preparation Time: 10 to 15 minutes, ongoing

Messiness Quotient: Medium

Materials: Old boxes and containers, colored masking tape

Why to try it: Working with blocks encourages cooperation, problem solving, and greater eye-hand coordination—among other things. Holding these large but lightweight blocks also gives the do-it-myself toddler the thrill of independence and capability.

How to do it: Need to clean out an old closet or your pantry? Sit baby beside you and send the empty cardboard boxes you find his way. As you pull out sturdy boxes, wrap them tightly with colored masking tape both to close and decorate them, and to help the box stand up to baby abuse. Whenever you

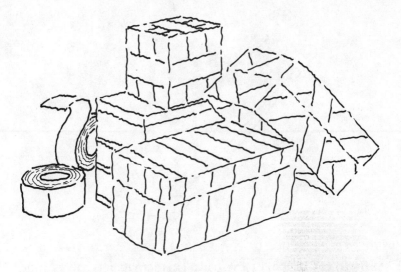

come across a box with an interesting shape, add it to the pile; when the pile gets too big, toss out your blocks and start over.

ROLL BALLS DOWNHILL

For quick fun, try this ball race course for babies.

Suggested Ages: Nine months and up

Your Child's Special Skills and Interests: Baby should be sitting up steadily, interested in ball play.

Preparation Time: 5 minutes

Messiness Quotient: Very low

Materials: Wooden board, 5 inches wide and 3 feet long; soft, lightweight ball about 6 inches in diameter

Commonsense Caution: Watch out for breakables when the ball starts rolling.

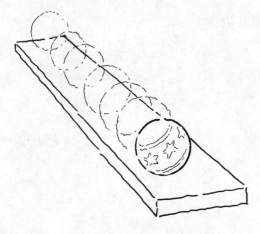

Why to try it: Babies love balls. This activity lets babies under one enjoy ball play and can teach toddlers gravity in action.

How to do it: Set baby in front of the board, and position yourself at the other end. Now lift the board to let your ball roll down to baby. She can pick it up and throw it back, roll it back, or even try to reverse the ramp and send the ball spinning down to you. Experiment with holding the board at different angles as you play and show baby how pitch affects speed.

Older-Baby Variations: If you have stairs, fashion a baby pitching machine of sorts. Let baby throw the ball up the stairs, then watch it tumble back down to her. You can also play this game outside, with a bowl of water at the end of a ramp. Baby will love watching the ball splash down in the water below. Or use a toy slide and a plastic baby doll or animal: Give it a splash bath, dry it off, and start again.

MAKE A BABY PRINT

A fun printing exercise to capture the impression of your baby's hands and feet.

Suggested Ages: Nine months and up

Your Child's Special Skills and Interests: Sitting steadily

Preparation Time: 10 minutes

Messiness Quotient: High

Materials: Sponge, washable tempera paint,
shallow bowl, paper

Commonsense Caution: If your baby's hands
immediately go to her mouth, she is likely to get
paint on her face and possibly in her eyes in this

exercise. Have wet cloths handy to wipe fingers
before they get to the face.

Why to try it: Young children love seeing how they can impact their world. This hands-on experience lets them put their
prints all over it. If you get some good handprints—a real feat
with squirmy fingers—turn them into cards and memorabilia
for relatives.

How to do it: Place a sponge in a shallow bowl and pour
washable paint over it. Now let your little one poke and press
the sponge with his fingers—it will help if you do this as well.
Show him how to make his prints on another piece of paper.
He can stamp his hand- and fingerprints, or practice preliminary finger painting with his paint-covered fingers.

No-Mess Variation: Wet fingers on a piece of construction
paper won't make a lasting mark, but the activity will occupy
a baby or toddler for a few fun minutes. Simply dampen baby's
fingers on a water-soaked sponge and then let him poke, press,
and draw with his wet digits on a lightly colored piece of paper
where the wetness will show as dark streaks and dots until it
evaporates. There is, of course, a dual purpose to this activity:
Baby will have happily cleaned his fingers without even knowing it.

PUT UP YOUR TEDDY BEARS

Pull down on a rope to raise a stuffed bear.

Suggested Ages: 9 months and up (with help); 18 months
on own

Your Child's Special Skills and Interests: Sitting or standing, able
to pull firmly on a rope

Preparation Time: 5 minutes

Messiness Quotient: Low

Materials: Rope, teddy bear, plastic bucket with handle

Commonsense Caution: Never leave a child alone with a rope; remove the rope immediately when you have finished playing this game, and never secure the rope to a fixed location.

Why to try it: As babies emerge from their initial state of almost complete helplessness, they love activities that let them actually do something. (And even if they can do virtually nothing, they'll love watching this activity.) Toddlers, the original do-it-yourselfers, love projects like this one.

How to do it: Toss a rope over a closet pole, a tree, or an inside or outside balcony. Tie the other end of the rope to a bucket, and put the teddy bear inside. Now show baby how pulling on the other end of the rope raises the bear into the sky. With help and direction, even infants can manage to pull on the rope. If you will be hoisting your bear to a second floor, you might station another adult at the top to receive the bucket, have him or her remove the bear and send down something else.

Teddy Bear Lover's Alternative: Some children may become upset by watching their teddy bear go for a ride, even if you assure them that the bear enjoys it. If this is the case, give something else, less beloved, a ride: an apple, a towel—or let your child put in his own choice of items as a surprise.

PLAY HIDE AND SEEK

Games that help your baby look and find.

Suggested Ages: All—but especially nine months to three years (and up)

Suggested Skill Level: Sitting up

Preparation Time: None

Messiness Quotient: Low to medium

Materials: Paper cups, socks, blankets, pillowcases, empty tissue boxes

Why to try it: From Peek-a-boo with babies to Hide and Seek with older toddlers, things that are hidden and reappear remain magical to the under (and over) three set, who may have only just recently learned that things they can't see continue to exist. But be aware that playing any kind of hiding game with the under-three set is decidedly different from what you may remember as an older child. Young children may feel very hidden just by covering their own eyes. They may tell you exactly where they are going as they set off to hide. They may deliberately not see what they are looking for just to extend the game. Try to follow their rules, however nonsensical they may seem. Competitive game playing will come soon enough to your family's life.

How to do it: Always be on the lookout for things you can hide and then pull out with a flourish of surprise. This could be as simple as popping out your thumb from a clenched fist for a very little baby, to putting a toy under a cup on the high chair for a six-month-old. As your baby becomes a toddler, games can become more advanced. Try these versions:

- Hide something inside a sock or pillowcase: Babies will busy themselves simply trying to get the object out; older toddlers can be encouraged to feel the object to try to guess what it is.

- Put one edge of a sheet or blanket at the top of a door and then close the door to anchor it in place. Now let your walking baby hide behind this hanging blanket and then pop out to "surprise" you. (*Commonsense Caution:* Take down the blanket immediately when you are done playing—hanging sheets could pose a strangling hazard to the unsupervised toddler.)

- Wear your hiding places: Stick items inside a pocket and help your baby feel it through your clothing, or challenge a toddler to find it. Better yet, hide something in one of their pockets, and sneak in a tickle or a hug when you retrieve it. If you enjoy sewing, you might even cut out half

a dozen pockets out of old or thrift-store clothes and sew them onto an old shirt for you to wear just for playing this game, or attach them to a blanket for a crawling baby to crawl around on and search.

- Put something that rattles inside a box: Toddlers can shake, rattle, and roll the box to try to hear what is making the sound; babies can simply be inspired to learn how to open the box to get inside.

- Look through a tunnel: Play Peek-a-boo with a cardboard paper towel tube or wrapping-paper tube. Or surreptitiously put a ball or other object inside the tube and roll it down to surprise baby at the other end.

❧ Tissue box hide-away: Turn an empty tissue box that has the circular opening for tissues onto its side, and drive a little car (or walk a little doll) inside through the arched hole where the tissues used to come out. Where did it go? Your baby or toddler will love reaching inside to find out. If your tissue box has only a rectangular opening at the top, let your kids reach in through this hole to find out what you've hidden inside. The thrill of reaching your hand into the unknown makes this terribly exciting for toddlers.

TRACE SOME TEXTURES

Toy boards for kids to trace with their fingers.

Suggested Ages: One year to 18 months

Skill Level: Sitting up, working on fine motor skills

Preparation Time: 20 minutes

Messiness Quotient: Low

The Sibling Factor: See Older-Child Variations below for ideas.

Materials: Self-adhesive or regular felt, sandpaper, carpet scraps, glue, double-sided tape, sturdy cardboard, scissors

Why to try it: Touch is still a primary sense for your child, who may also be beginning to become entranced with moving his fingers along a line in order to track a design. This activity combines new textures with finger tracing.

How to do it: Make tracing texture boards by cutting designs into pieces of differently textured materials and then gluing or taping them onto a sturdy cardboard. Your child will enjoy either tracing the smooth cardboard surface in between the

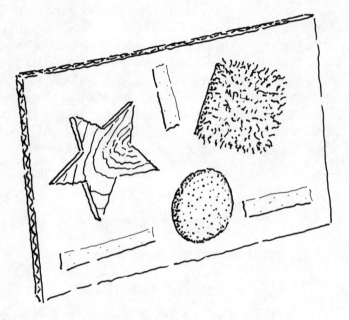

textures, or tracing the textured surface surrounded by card-board. You can also make a sticky surface for touching and tracing by applying double-sided tape to a piece of cardboard, or add an extra dimension of fun by attaching the textures to a piece of plastic mirror so your child can watch his fingers as they move across the surface.

Older-Child Variations: As your child approaches two and a half or three, you might make another set of these boards, designed like simple mazes that she follows with her fingers. Or you might even let your near two- or three-year-old make her own boards: Give her a small pool of white glue and an ear swab, a piece of construction paper, and a pile of wagon-wheel-shaped pasta. She can glue them onto the paper as she wishes, then she can trace the spaces in between with her fingers or make an elaborate design with a marker between the shapes.

PLAY FOOTSIE

Make a feely foot path for children to experience with their toes.

Suggested Ages: 18 months and up

Your Child's Special Skills and Interests: Experienced walkers only, exploring touch with feet

Preparation Time: 15 minutes

Messiness Quotient: High

Materials: Shallow pie pans or metal baking dishes, water, and a selection of flour, cooked pasta, uncooked oatmeal, crackers, prepared gelatin, corn starch, oil, or other weird substances you can walk on

Commonsense Caution: Children can slip as they walk through the different textures. Be sure to watch them closely.

Why to try it: Shortly after they begin to walk, children love to feel different textures under their bare feet. Indulge this instinct with a sensory footpath, perfect outside on a warm summer day or, if you are brave about messes and desperately in the throes of cabin fever, feasible indoors on a floor you can mop.

How to do it: Give your child a full range of sensory experiences right under her feet. Set out shallow pans filled with everything from cooked pasta and gelatin to crackers or a gooey mix of cornstarch and water. In between each particularly messy substance, put a shallow pan of water for a quick rinse and a manmade puddle splash. For variety, color the water in different pans with food coloring, and fill some of the pans with cool water and some of them with warm. Plan plenty of time for this project: Most kids will want to walk this course again and again.

Less Messy Variation: Just make an outdoor puddle splash course with shallow plastic tubs filled with water to splash in (also possible indoors, on towels). Or, try a non-messy texture course: Let your baby walk a path of carpet and vinyl squares (get samples at the flooring store) as well as pieces of board, or use textures such as cotton balls or rice glued to cardboard squares. As she walks, talk about what each square feels like under her toes.

ARRANGE STUFF

Teach your baby how to construct by connecting items, rather than stacking them.

Suggested Ages: 18 months and up

Your Child's Special Skills and Interests: Working on fine motor skills

Preparation Time: 5 minutes

Messiness Quotient: Low

The Sibling Factor: While your young child sticks away haphazardly, help your older child make a real flower arrangement or an arrangement of homemade paper flowers.

Materials: Floral foam; dried grasses, flowers, sticks, pencils, or straws

Commonsense Caution: Keep floral foam out of the hands of children still inclined to put things in their mouths.

Why to try it: This is an exercise in hand-eye coordination, tactile sensation, and artistic inspiration. It is also a great way to use those blocks of floral foam that came with the arrangements you received when your baby was born.

How to do it: During your daily walk outside, bring along a piece of floral foam and let your little one stick all the dried flowers, sticks, rocks, and other treasured finds into the foam as a kind of found-art display. If you are stuck indoors, make an arrangement of pencils, toothpicks, toothbrushes, and anything else you can find that will stick into the foam.

HAVE FUN WITH COOKIE CUTTERS

Try some cookie cutter crafts without the cookies.

Suggested Ages: 18 months and up

Your Child's Special Skills and Interests: Able to hold a brush and a cookie cutter

Preparation Time: 10 minutes

Messiness Quotient: Medium—paint is involved.

The Sibling Factor: An older child might want to print cards or wrapping paper with these same tools.

Materials: Cookie cutters, washable paints and paintbrushes, paper; potatoes, knife, and washable stamp pads

Why to try it: Using cookie cutters as a guide, young children can make accurate paintings and prints of shapes and objects.

How to do it: While you hold the cookie cutter on a piece of paper, let your child paint or color with markers on the inside of the shape. When you lift the cutter, she'll delight in the picture she's made on the paper. Cookie cutters are also the easiest way to make potato prints. Cut a potato in half, then imprint the cutter into a cut half of the potato. Now go around the outside of the potato with a knife, cutting in on the sides to meet the point where the cookie-cutter imprint begins. Remove this excess and you'll have a potato printer within minutes, and your child can begin stamping away.

No-Stamp-Pad Variation: If you don't have a stamp pad or it is too dry to work effectively, an older child can paint or color with markers on the bottom of the potato stamps and make vibrant prints.

CARVE AND TRACE

An introduction to sculpting and engraving.

Suggested Ages: 18 months and up

Your Child's Special Skills and Interests: Able to hold a pencil or marker

Preparation Time: 5 minutes

Messiness Quotient: Medium—cutting foam can make crumbs.

The Sibling Factor: Once a design has been carved, the bottom of the foam around the carving can be painted, flipped over, and used as a stamp. The places that are carved will not show up on paper.

Materials: Styrofoam or floral foam, plastic spoon, marker

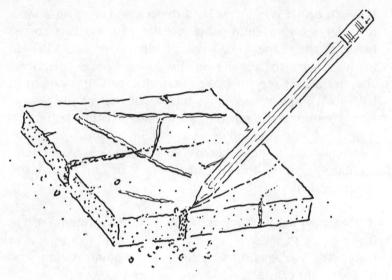

Commonsense Caution: If you try this with a
plastic knife—which two- and three-year-olds
love—be sure to supervise them constantly.

Why to try it: This exercise teaches practical skills like holding a marker to draw letters and learning how to better use
knives and spoons.

How to do it: A piece of Styrofoam offers an interesting surface on which to draw and can help toddlers "feel" how to
make certain shapes. Pressing down hard with a marker, "en-
grave" some of the letters and shapes your baby is currently
learning. Then let baby move his pen in the same grooves—
and dig a few of his own. Floral foam also offers a great surface
for toddlers who are becoming advanced in their use of cutlery.
Let your older toddler (two years and up) have the thrill of
really cutting something by giving him a plastic knife and let-

ting him saw through floral foam. If even plastic serration makes you nervous (and plastic knives can cut, though not seriously), give him a spoon and let him dig away.

FINGER-PAINT!

Tips on basic finger painting.

Suggested ages: 18 months and up

Your Child's Special Skills and Interests: Highly tactile, but has stopped putting hands in mouth; not afraid of having messy things on hands

Preparation Time: 10 minutes

Messiness Quotient: High

Materials: Liquid starch, powdered tempera paint, wax paper

> **Commonsense Caution:** If babies are too young or too oral for this project, they will try to eat the paint on their hands, or wipe it off. Many young children prefer painting with brushes to having paint on their hands.

Why to try it: This is an experiment in color and touch sensation—and great fun for your toddler.

How to do it: Put a towel or newspaper under a table. Tape waxed paper (wax side up) to the surface where your child will work. If the paper is on a roll, let one end of the roll hang down the side so that when necessary you can rip off the painted part and pull up fresh paper to paint on. Now sprinkle a little dry paint on the paper (put different colors in different locations) and squeeze some liquid starch across the paint. Show baby

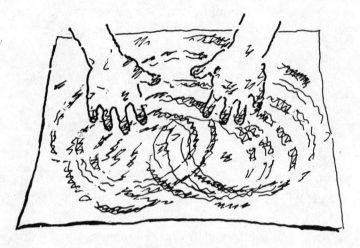

how to use her hands to mix the two together to create wild designs and colors. For ease of cleanup, consider stripping baby to the diaper before painting, and have a sink bath ready nearby: Just lift her up and dip when you are done. This is also a great activity to do outside in warm weather. Hose down the surface and put baby in her wading pool for a bath.

Store-Bought Variations: There are many different recipes for finger paints, as well as a wide array of store-bought varieties. The homemade versions are usually cheaper in the long run and are often more fun, since you get the fun of mixing them up yourself.

RUN AN OBSTACLE COURSE

Make a homemade gymnasium that lets kids use their large muscles and energy.

Suggested Ages: 18 months and up

Your Child's Special Skills and Interests: Walking, running, jumping

Preparation Time: 15 minutes

Messiness Quotient: Medium—you'll have to put everything back.

Materials: Pillows, balls, couch cushions, ride-on toys (Sit-n-Spins, plastic slides, etc.), tunnels (cardboard boxes or store-bought version)

Commonsense Caution: Running a course with built-in obstacles sometimes causes spills along with thrills.

Why to try it: Let your toddler practice the toddler triathlon—running, spinning, and jumping—with this activity, which usually lasts all morning long. It also makes nap time a breeze for your child *and* you.

How to do it: Scatter the pillows and cushions around the house to establish the course. In between the pillows, station cars to drive, slides to scoot down, balls to roll into bottomless coffee cans turned on their side, and open cardboard boxes or store-bought tunnels to crawl through. If you'd like to try this with a crawling child, simply lower the obstacles and remove those above her skill level, then show her the course by letting her follow you around it.

PRETEND TO BE ANIMALS

Exercise the natural way.

Suggested Ages: 18 months and up

Your Child's Special Skills and Interests: Walking, running, hopping

Preparation Time: None

Messiness Quotient: None

Materials: None

Why to try it: To exercise your child's body and imagination, and your own.

How to do it: Look at pictures of animals in a book, and then figure out ways to make your body look and behave as the pictured animal does. Use the following exercises as starting points, then make up your own.

Roly-poly: Lie on your backs. Bring your knees to your chest, clasping them with your hands. Now rock back and forth from your shoulders to your buttocks. This not only stretches your spine, it makes you look like a round little roly-poly.

Butterfly Wings: Sit with your feet flat together. Now move your knees up and down, flapping them like butterfly wings and stretching out the inside of your thighs.

Fly like a Bird: Standing up, reach your hands above your head and place them back to back. Now gracefully bring them down and up, down and up, imagining yourself winging your way across the sky.

Elephant Trunk: From the standing position of bird, bend at the waist and drop your arms down in front of you. Now clasp them together to form an elephant's trunk. Swing slowly from side to side, just as an elephant swings its trunk as it walks.

Frog Hop: This one's self-explanatory—and will surely be one of your child's favorites.

Giraffe Stretch: How high can you and your child reach? How long and tall can you stretch your necks? Your limitations are obvious, but it's fun to try.

Variations: Once you've tried as many animal antics as you can think up, try imitating some inanimate objects. Almost as soon as they can walk and run, toddlers love to fly like airplanes and chug like trains. A two-year-old can even engage in a rudimentary game of charades. Take turns making shapes and objects with your body. At first, you can tell your child what to do. As he gets more experienced, you can introduce the concept of guessing the shape you are making.

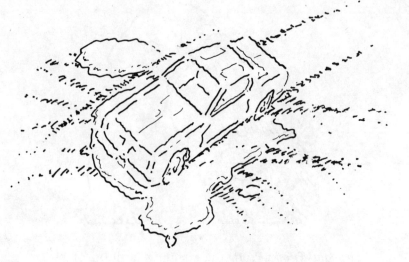

PAINT WITH YOUR CARS

Turn tiny cars into artistic tools.

Suggested Ages: 18 months and up

Your Child's Special Skills and Interests: Interested and able to
roll cars around

Preparation Time: 5 minutes

Messiness Quotient: High

The Sibling Factor: You'll need a car for everybody,
but be aware: This activity may become nearly
impossible to supervise or contain with more than
one child.

Materials: Washable paint, tiny cars, large pieces of paper, tape,
shallow pan

Why to try it: This activity is more about effect than result:
By running his car through puddles of paint, your child can

see how paint is spread over a surface and how the implement doing the spreading—in this case, a tiny toy car—makes a difference in the end product.

How to do it: Cover the work surface with taped-down paper and the floor with a towel or other drop cloth. Now pour little puddles of paint around the paper, and let your toddler—and his toy—do the rest as he drives his vehicle through puddles and around and around in circles. If you have trucks or cars with actual treads, so much the better. When the painting fun is over, fill a shallow pie pan with water and let your toddler take his toys on another drive—through the car wash.

No-Car Variations: Think about the bottoms of other plastic toys you might use as art supplies. Paint the bottom of a rubber frog's feet and have it "hop" across the paper, for instance.

HOP TO IT!

An indoor jump course.

Suggested Ages: 18 months and up

Your Child's Special Skills and Interests: Walking, learning shapes and colors

Preparation Time: 10 minutes

Messiness Quotient: Low

Materials: Butcher-block paper, or a dozen sheets of construction or copy paper, masking tape, markers

Why to try it: Exercise your toddler's brain and body at the same time with this easy-to-do game.

How to do it: Tape a 6-foot length of butcher-block paper to the floor, or tape a dozen pieces of paper to the floor, scattered

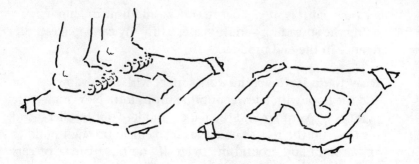

over a 6-foot span. On each individual sheet (or spread out over the butcher-block paper) draw one large shape, number, letter, or color that your child knows or that you are currently teaching her. Now, turn her loose at the beginning of the course. Can she jump to the heart? The square? The letter "A"? Once she gets the hang of this, ask her to put a hand on the heart or to sit on the green circle. Children can usually run the course again and again and may enjoy a drawing session at the end, tracing over the shapes you have drawn with their own washable (in case they skid off onto the floor) marker.

Outdoor Variation: You can also play this game outdoors, by marking the shapes with chalk on a sidewalk or driveway. Be sure to add challenges by specifying a shape and a color, or by writing letters or numbers.

PAINT WITH MARBLES

Painting with marbles.

Suggested Ages: Two years old and up

Your Child's Special Skills and Interests: Is playing with small objects but is not oral

Preparation Time: 5 minutes

Messiness Quotient: Medium to high

Materials: Unpainted wooden beads (available from craft shops)
or marbles, paper, muffin tin, washable paint,
2-inch-deep baking pan, tape, spoon

Commonsense Caution: Not for use with children who put small objects in their mouth.

Why to try it: This sort of painting keeps hands quite clean and can produce beautiful beads and designs.

How to do it: Tape your paper in the baking pan. Squirt different-colored paints into the cups in the muffin pan. Drop marbles into each cup. Now scoop each marble out of the paint with a spoon and put it on the pan with the paper in the bottom. Tip the pan back and forth and let the marble roll around on the paper, painting it with marvelous designs. If you have them available, you can also let large unpainted wooden beads do the rolling—and end up with beautifully marbled beads for you and your baby to string.

SEE HOW YOU MEASURE UP

Measuring with sticks, blocks, and string.

Suggested Ages: Two years and up

Your Child's Special Skills and Interests: Showing an interest in
size and comparing size

Preparation Time: 5 minutes

Messiness Quotient: Medium

Materials: Blocks, yarn or string, a straight tree
or bush branch

Why to try it: How big is it? How tall is it? Such concerns are compelling for many toddlers and preschoolers. This activity helps them get answers in ways they understand.

How to do it: An inch or a foot means nothing to your child. But if you tell him that his desk is 25 building blocks long and let him see them lined up, he gets a much better idea of its size. Help your child get started taking the measure of things by using a roll of yarn, a piece of branch, a set of blocks, or even his own hand. As he lays things like this out along the distance he wants to measure, he will begin to get a clear sense of how big or small something is.

MAKE WEARABLE ART

*A way to turn your child's art into necklaces
and pins she can wear.*

Suggested Ages: Two years and up

Your Child's Special Skills and Interests: Drawing, beginning to
show pride in artwork

Preparation Time: 5 minutes

Messiness Quotient: Very low

Materials: Empty plastic name tag holders on a chain or pinned
on, stick-on plastic name tags, and a variety of drawing or
painting supplies, stickers, stamps, and paper

Commonsense Caution: Be careful of stickpins
when pinning on tags and only pin to outer lay-

ers; don't let children sleep wearing a necklace or
pinned-on nametag.

Why to try it: As your child begins to appreciate her artistic prowess, you can give her work bigger play than the refrigerator by allowing her to wear it wherever she goes.

How to do it: Give your child a piece of paper cut about the size of the plastic name tag holder, but taped to a bigger piece of paper in case her drawing goes over the edge. Now let her draw, paint, or decorate to her heart's content. When she has finished, slip her drawing into the plastic holder and pin it to her coat, sweater, hat, or other outside layer of clothing so she can share it with everyone she sees. You won't want to pin it to clothing that lies against her skin in case the pin becomes unhooked. If you don't have a plastic name tag holder, you can have your child draw with markers on store-bought name

tag stickers (or cut-up pieces of adhesive shelving paper) and stick them onto her shirt.

PLAY WITH BEANS, BEADS, AND BUTTONS

How to play with the tiny beads and buttons tiny fingers love.

Suggested Ages: Two years and up

Your Child's Special Skills and Interests: Interested in picking up tiny objects but not putting them in his mouth

Preparation Time: 10 minutes

Messiness Quotient: Medium to high—beans and beads love to roll around on the floor.

Materials: Seven-bean-soup beans, beads, empty pill or film containers, egg carton or muffin tin, clear plastic tubing (¾ inch, available at all hardware stores), play dough, flat toothpicks, Styrofoam

> **Commonsense Caution:** These activities are only for children who have completely stopped putting non-edible things in their mouths. Even so, you should never leave any young child unsupervised when playing these games.

Why to try it: As toddlers continue to develop their fine motor skills and begin to be able to understand the concepts of counting and colors, matching and sorting, patterns and sequencing, a bag of multi-colored beads, buttons, or beans becomes a marvelous toy in the following games.

How to do it: There are dozens of ways to play with beads, buttons, or beans—many of which your child has yet to invent. Here are a few to get him started:

Roller Coaster Ride: Threading beads onto sturdy twine is a great hand-eye and fine motor exercise, but remains challenging for children under three. An easier (and more fun) alternative is to pour the beans, beads, buttons, or dry, round or O-shaped cereal for the still oral child into a wide, shallow bowl and let your toddler select from them and drop them individually into a piece of clear plastic tubing (about ¾ inch in diameter, 3 feet long). Once he's dropped a bunch of beads inside, your toddler can help you move the tubing up and down and twist it into big loops, which makes the beads zip around inside like a little roller coaster. When it's time for cleanup, or just to start over, simply tilt the tubing and let the beads empty out into your original bowl.

First Impressions: Bring out the beads or buttons during your next play-dough session and show your toddler how to use them to make "cool" impressions in the dough. Why does this keep her busy for so long? Because she has to test every single button to see what impression it will leave in the dough.

Sort It Out: Muffin tins, egg cartons, film canisters: All of these make great containers for a toddler's collection of beads or buttons. He can busy himself all morning transferring the beads and buttons from a jar or bowl into the other containers. This activity also allows you to begin to introduce your child to sorting according to size, shape, and color—concepts that math teachers say are the underpinnings of early math literacy and a preliminary understanding of data and statistics. Of course, these understandings don't come immediately. Don't be surprised if your child sorts according to his own, possibly incomprehensible, system for quite a while.

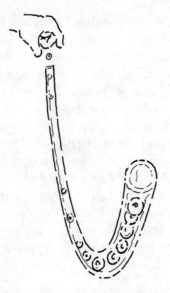

Buttonholed: With a block of Styrofoam (from craft stores, or use what you sometimes get as packing material) a bag of buttons and some flat, rounded-end toothpicks can give toddlers an early experience in threading the needle. Show them how to use the toothpick to stick the button onto the Styrofoam. It's a simple activity and has absolutely no ultimate product, but most kids love the feel of sticking the toothpicks into the foam and experiencing the success of nabbing the button.

MAKE HOMEMADE CLAY

Recipes for three make-at-home play clays.

Suggested Ages: Two years and up

Preparation Time: 20 minutes for each clay

Messiness Quotient: High

Materials: Flake detergent (such as Ivory); cornstarch, sand; flour, salt, cream of tartar, food coloring, water; saucepan

> **Commonsense Caution:** Younger babies may
> like to eat clay as well as feel it, so limit their play
> until this impulse is under control.

Why to try it: Mixing and pouring and kneading are toddler passions, which these recipes indulge while putting them to good use. The dough is often cheaper than the kind you buy, and making it yourself extends the activity and the fun by a good half hour. Be sure to let your child help measure ingredients, and later play with fitting the dough in and out of containers: Such exercises help your child develop a preliminary understanding of measurement, an important math skill.

Classic Clay: One-half cup salt, one cup white flour, one cup water, and a teaspoon each of cream of tartar and vegetable oil. Mix everything in a pan and cook it on low, stirring until a ball forms. The result: a product surprisingly like—if not better than—the stuff you can buy. You can add your own scents and colors if you wish while you knead the ball, and it keeps for what seems like forever in a covered plastic container.

Soap Dough: Use this dough to make a snowman that will never melt. Just add two cups of Ivory Snow to one-half cup water and whip with an electric mixer (you and your child can hold the mixer together). Then form the mixture into three balls, press them together with toothpick anchors in between, and presto: your own snowman, ready to decorate. No need to use coal on this snowman—real buttons work perfectly well.

Feel Dough: Try this activity outside where you have a hose to wash the whole area down afterward. Simply fill a wide bowl with two cups of cornstarch and add one cup of water and mix. Then let your child dig in with her hands. This dough—which you really can't make anything with—is wonderfully weird. Let your child try to pick up a handful and make a ball. Just as she finishes molding it, the whole enterprise will "melt" right through her fingers. The same thing happens when you poke at it with your finger: First it is hard, then your finger just slips right into the goo.

PLAY SCIENTIST

Easy experiments with gravity and flotation.

Suggested Ages: Two years and up

Your Child's Special Skills and Interests: Dropping things

Preparation Time: 10 minutes

Messiness Quotient: High

Materials: Towel, plastic or metal bowl; various light, heavy, and floatable objects

Why to try it: A little parent-sanctioned dropping and splashing play is a welcome break from rules for most toddlers.

How to do it: Set up a testing station in your kitchen or bathroom, or outside. Put a towel out on the floor, and set an unbreakable bowl full of water on top. From nearby cabinets and drawers grab a dozen or so objects, choosing them according to whether your child still puts things in his mouth. The following objects are fun: a bar of soap, a crayon, a paper clip, plastic cup, sponge, ice cube, pencil, piece of paper, set of keys, rubber band, turkey baster, metal spoon. Now encourage your child to test each object, dropping it into the water to see if it sinks or floats. Can he sink the floating objects by pushing them down? Which objects make the biggest splash when they hit the water? Once you are done experimenting with water, move on to the concept of gravity. Empty the water from the bowl, and let your child drop the same objects into the bowl from a high chair or a standing position. Which object hits the bowl first when dropped? Which makes the loudest sound? The softest? Do different objects fall differently? In addition to the objects above, try dropping a feather, a cotton ball, a piece of paper scrunched into a ball, and a flat piece of paper.

Chapter Two

~~~~~~~~~~

MEAL TIMES

Fun, Learning, and Nutrition

As any parent of a baby old enough to eat solids already knows, meal times aren't just about eating. Eating solids opens the door to an entirely new sensory universe for babies, from tasting food and feeling its texture in their mouths, to feeling and exploring it with their fingers. For neat and tidy first-time parents, this new stage may require that you increase your comfort level with messiness. At such times, it helps to remember how educational eating really is for children. Babies learn about the varying degrees of solidity by trying to pick up a handful of yogurt with their bare hands, and about what rolls and what doesn't when they push around a piece of O-shaped cereal or a scrap of bread. They also learn about temperatures, textures—even gravity, as they drop pieces of cereal, one by one, off the edge of their high chair.

Your goals during your baby's meal times should be to make sure he doesn't choke because he's stuffed too much food in his mouth and to ensure that a modicum of nutrition does reach its intended destination. Then sit back and watch your baby, the original natural scientist, experiment with his food. Once you feel comfortable with this process, you might even start offering him the edible projects in this chapter for meal-time testing.

Of course, meal time isn't only about eating and playing with food. It is also about preparing it. Little cooks can be both great helps and great hindrances to your progress in the kitchen. However beneficial your child's help is, including him or her will take a little planning and imagination on your part and may seem to slow the whole cooking process down. And for parents of more than one child, this might be true. Too many cooks in the kitchen can simply be too many cooks in the kitchen. But if you have only one young assistant, using him as cheap help may ultimately pay off. Besides, a baby who isn't included in what you are doing may find ways to get your attention that end up being much more time-consuming than it would have been to have just let him help.

Meal Preparation as Parent-Child Activity

Ironically, you may find that even though you feel too busy to really cook, recipes that are more elaborate are actually easier to do with a child at your side because they include processes that allow one to participate. This is especially true if you simply look at the meal preparation as part of your parent-child activity time and give yourself the time to make homemade biscuits that baby can help roll and cut or to make a spinach salad that baby can help wash and dry. Once you start looking for kid-friendly steps in recipes, you may find yourself making things from scratch you wouldn't have tried before baby came along. You will need to help your short assistant reach the work area, however. You can purchase or build her a wide bench that puts her a bit above counter height when she is standing or let her work at her own, kid-size table. For some not strictly cooking-related tasks, you can also let her work on the floor. Throw a towel or a plastic tablecloth in an out-of-traffic corner of the kitchen and get her started working at easily contained on-the-towel tasks like wrapping things in foil, washing vegetables, spinning salad, and so forth.

Turn Kitchen Tools into Toys

In addition to trying new recipes with baby, you may also find yourself considering small kitchen appliances you wouldn't have bought before, simply because they offer fun ways for baby to cook with you. A child of two years old, for instance, can help you squeeze fresh juice on a juicer, and at less than that age children are happy to scoop ice and salt into the sides of a homemade ice cream maker. Other kitchen tools that become toys when a child is your assistant cook include a mortar and pestle (even a child of a year and a half can grind up herbs this way), a salad spinner, a crank apple peeler/corer, and an old-fashioned crank coffee grinder. Even a simple task like putting the beaters into your unplugged electric hand mixer can be a treat for you both, as you cook and clean and your child slowly but surely matches the beater with the hole it goes into. All of these tools-turned-toys actively involve baby in food preparation, but at a safe distance.

And safety is, of course, a primary concern when a child is your assistant chef. The kitchen is full of hazards: knives, burners and hot dishes, glasses that can break. As you cook, keep in mind that you don't want junior directly under your feet while you are working at the stove: Even tripping just a little could send scalding food onto baby below. You'll also want to keep hot dishes on the back burners where baby can't reach up and pull them off the stove, and be sure to physically block off the oven area if this gets dangerously hot to the touch on the outside. Knives, glassware, and other potentially sharp hazards should naturally be kept well out of baby's reach. Once you've removed obvious dangers, keep a close eye on baby, and get cooking!

WHAT TO DO WITH BABY WHILE YOU COOK

BRING BABY ALONG

Introduce chef baby to your kitchen.

Suggested Ages: Birth to nine months

Your Child's Special Skills and Interests: Sitting in an infant seat or on own, not walking or crawling

Preparation Time: None

Messiness Quotient: None

Materials: None

Why to try it: You are the most interesting entertainment possible for baby, especially when you are doing things that make noise and use different shiny tools.

How to do it: Give baby a seat of honor in your kitchen where he can see all that goes on but is safely removed from hot or sharp objects. Then spotlight your kitchen work, keeping in mind how exciting the blur of whirling colors in a blender would be to a baby who has never seen anything like it, how mesmerizing steam from a pot would look, or how amazing a broken egg really is. If this inspires you to more complex cooking with baby, so much the better. But even if you only make a grilled cheese sandwich, baby will enjoy hearing you explain how the bread has turned from white to brown, or watching you pull the bread apart to show the melted cheese.

PLAY KITCHEN TOOL PEEK-A-BOO

Turning funnels and other kitchen tools into toys.

Suggested Ages: Three months and up

Your Child's Special Skills and Interests: Playing Peek-A-Boo

Preparation Time: None

Messiness Quotient: Low

Materials: Kitchen funnels, slotted spoons, colander

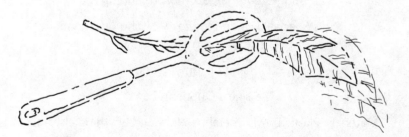

Why to try it: This simple game is easy for you and down-right magical for baby.

How to do it: Kitchen tools with holes offer quick opportunities for Peek-A-Boo with baby. Stick your finger through a funnel and wag it at baby, then quickly pull it back. Poke a long piece of grass or a feather, a stick or a pencil through the holes in a sieve or a slotted spoon, move it around, then yank it back for a quick retreat. Because babies haven't developed the concept of object permanence, when you pull the object back through the hole it will seem to them as though it has magically disappeared. In fact, just looking through holes at baby and then pulling your face away to "hide" is also quite intriguing for your child for the same reason.

SET THE KITCHEN SPINNING

Put a new spin on your same old kitchen utensils.

Suggested Ages: Six months and up

Your Child's Special Skills and Interests: Sitting up, mesmerized by spinning objects

Preparation Time: None

Messiness Quotient: Low

Materials: Plastic bowls, metal pan lids, and anything else you can spin around

Commonsense Caution: Don't spin anything that baby could grab and accidentally eat or otherwise hurt himself with.

Why to try it: Watching something spin around will keep your baby occupied for a few minutes and will give you just enough time to get that pot off the stove.

How to do it: The hard floor in most kitchens is just perfect for spinning. With baby sitting not too far away, set any number of common kitchen objects going round and round: a pot lid, a bowl, a plastic cup, a wooden spoon, even a book with a slippery cover. You'll be surprised at how many things do spin on a hard floor once you attempt it. Many babies will sit and watch in amazement as the spinning object slowly stops, becoming not a blur but a single object. You can also set objects in a salad spinner, put the top on and spin, then lift the top off so baby can look at the spinning things inside. And if you have a portable Lazy Susan, you are in luck. Set it in front of baby, put his rattle on top, and spin it around where he can reach it. If he puts it back down on the Lazy Susan, spin it back around where you can pick it up.

LET BABY STIR

A not so messy baby-as-baker experience.

Suggested Ages: Nine months and up

Your Child's Special Skills and Interests: Stirring, imitating cooking

Preparation Time: 5 minutes

Messiness Quotient: Medium to high

Materials: Old spice jars half-filled with flour, plastic bowls, wooden spoons, floor covering such as a beach towel

Why to try it: The real flour gives an authentic touch to this pretend activity, but without quite the mess.

How to do it: Provide your child with several old spice shakers half-filled with flour, some wooden spoons, and plastic bowls. Let her shake and stir away while she sits on the floor. When she has finished her "baking," put the flour she's shaken out in the bowl back into the shakers for next time and throw the towel in the wash.

Extra-Sensory Variation: Fill your old spice jars with a small amount of spices: dill, tarragon, basil, thyme, marjoram—any spice that isn't hot (do not include cayenne or curry, for example). Then let your child shake, mix, stir, and smell. You can also fill the jars with various colored sugars (make your own with your child by mixing white granulated sugar with food coloring) and for shaking into the bowl—or on top of cakes and cookies.

DECORATE THE TABLE

Turn your kitchen table into a young artist's dream canvas.

Suggested Ages: One year and up

Your Child's Special Skills and Interests: Interested and able to draw on own

Preparation Time: 10 minutes

Messiness Quotient: High

The Sibling Factor: This can be a good family project as long as older children can be understanding when toddlers accidentally scribble on their careful drawings.

Materials: Butcher-block paper (or paper bags turned inside out),
markers or crayons, tape, scissors

Why to try it: The expanse of your kitchen table covered with
paper is downright inspirational to nearly every young artist,
keeping him busy and within view while you cook.

How to do it: Cover your kitchen table or breakfast bar with
long rolls of white butcher-block paper or brown paper bags
cut open and turned inside out. Tape the paper's edges down.
Now tell your child to "decorate" the table for dinner and give
him washable markers or crayons and let him loose.

LET YOUR LITTLE MONSTER, MASH

Get out extra energy—and juice at the same time.

Suggested Ages: One year and up

Your Child's Special Skills and Interests: Mashing things

Preparation Time: 3 minutes

Messiness Quotient: Low—unless she breaks open the fruit

Materials: A potato masher, a medium-ripe lemon or orange, a
plastic bowl

Why to try it: Let your toddler indulge in some parent-
approved mashing, just for the fun of it.

How to do it: Arm your child with an old-fashioned potato
masher and a medium-ripe lemon or orange. Show her how to
push down on the fruit to "mash" it in the bowl. She'll be able
to have very little impact on the fruit at first, of course, but
she'll have fun trying. As she gets older and more adept at using

the potato masher, let her use it to mash things that really need mashing, including for instance, a baked potato. Just be sure to put a towel under the bowl to contain the mess if real mashing is going to occur. And if you plan to serve this mashed potato, make sure that your little masher has clean hands and that you watch the mashing closely.

GIVE YOUR MEAL THE BRUSH-OFF

Basting and painting are one and the same to baby.

Suggested Ages: 18 months and up

Your Child's Special Skills and Interests: Able to wield a paintbrush

Preparation Time: 5 minutes

Messiness Quotient: Medium

The Sibling Factor: There's probably not room in your kitchen for two buttery paintbrush-wielding assistants.

Materials: Basting brush, marinade or melted warm butter or milk, bowl, towel

Commonsense Caution: Never let baby baste hot food. And because of the contamination issues connected with raw meat—especially poultry—baste these food products yourself. Raw egg dishes should also be avoided.

Why to try it: Your vegetables get coated with marinade and your baked goods with an even application of butter or milk; baby gets to have fun painting the coating on.

How to do it: Wash your hands and your baby's hands. Spread out an old towel on a low table, bench, or chair or on the kitchen floor in an out-of-the-way corner. Now put down a bowl of marinade or butter or milk, the items baby will be basting, and a basting brush on the towel. Show baby how to carefully coat the food with this kitchen brush, emphasizing that he should keep his fingers out off the food and marinade and staying by his side to make sure that he follows this rule. Once you start thinking about what baby can brush on food, you'll discover more possibilities. Let baby help you make homemade croutons out of old bread, for instance, by brushing on melted herbed butter on the squares of toast. Or have your toddler help with making pizza by brushing olive oil and pizza sauce on the crust.

GET TO THE GUTS OF THE MATTER

Let your kids dig in.

Suggested Ages: 18 months and up

Your Child's Special Skills and Interests: Digging

Materials: Pumpkins, squash, cucumbers, cantaloupe, tomatoes; plastic or wooden spoons

Preparation Time: None

Messiness Quotient: Medium to high

Commonsense Caution: Watch closely to make sure your child doesn't try to eat the vegetable "guts."

Why to try it: Vegetables are squishy, slimy, and full of seeds; gutting them is kid's work—and play.

How to do it: When squash or another seeded fruit or vegetable is on the menu, be sure to let your toddler in on the dirty work of pulling out the seeds. After you cut the fruit or vegetable in two at a safe distance from your toddler, hand him a spoon and let him help you scoop out the seeds and pulp into a waiting bowl. Once the scooping is done, roll up his sleeves and let him play with the "guts" of the vegetable while you explain a little about seeds. If you want to take this lesson a step further, take a few of the seeds and put them on a damp paper towel rolled inside a glass jar or on a wet sponge. Keep the towel or sponge consistently damp and watch for the seeds to sprout in a few days.

TURN OVER A NEW LEAF

They may not eat salad, but they'll help you make it.

Suggested Ages: 18 months and up

Your Child's Special Skills and Interests: Ripping things apart, washing things

Preparation Time: 5 minutes

Messiness Quotient: Medium

The Sibling Factor: Two kids means two salad spinners or two siblings very good at taking turns.

Materials: Greens for your salad, medium-size bath towel, bowl of water, paper towels or salad spinner, trash can, salad bowl

Commonsense Caution: Because of the possibility of *E. coli* bacteria on fresh greens, you should wash your child's hands immediately after he or

she handles the greens, and you might even consider pre-washing the greens yourself before letting your child "help."

Why to try it: Salads are one of the few things your child can
make in the kitchen without heat or knives.

How to do it: Wash your hands and your child's hands. Now
fill a bowl half full with water and set it on a towel. Working
beside your child, put pieces of greens in the bowl and, using
both hands, swish them around in the water to clean them.
Now take them out one at a time and put them on paper towels
to pat dry, or in a salad spinner for you to spin (this part is
often too difficult for most pre-three-year-olds). For an extra
treat, take the top off the spinner at the end to watch the greens
spinning. Once the greens are clean, let your child help you
rip them into pieces for the salad.

Older-Child Variations: As you wash the additional salad
ingredients, play Sink or Float with your two- or three-year-
old. Will the tomato sink in a bowl or sink filled with water,
or will it float? Take turns guessing with your child as you wash.

PLAY MUFFIN MAN

Suggested Ages: 18 months and up

Your Child's Special Skills and Interests: Working toward being
able to hold small items pinched between the thumb and index
finger

Preparation Time: 3 minutes

Messiness Quotient: Low

The Sibling Factor: Two muffin pans and two stacks of liners
    should keep both children busy for a while.

Materials: Muffin pan, small stack of paper muffin-pan liners

Why to try it: Turning kitchen staples into toys puts a multitude of unusual playthings within easy reach and minimizes your cleanup at meal's end, because your "toy box" is as close as the nearest cabinet.

How to do it: Pull the muffin liners apart and put them in a row. Now show baby how to place them inside the muffin tin. As baby gets older, you can turn muffin-tin lining into a game that reinforces learning of shapes, colors, or letters or matching or patterning skills. Draw different shapes on half the liners and put them in the muffin cups; then have your child try to put the matching muffin shapes over the top. Or simply let your child sort a handful of muffin liners by color (most liners come in an assortment).

DECORATE THE MEAL

Finishing touches that make the meal fun.

Suggested Ages: Two years and up

Your Child's Special Skills and Interests: Fine motor control developed enough to squeeze bottles and sprinkle tiny amounts of food

Preparation Time: Variable

Messiness Quotient: Medium to high—little decorators can become aggressive.

Materials: Extra squeeze bottles or cake-decorating bags

Why to try it: Even in a gourmet restaurant, the extra flourishes on your plate that make your meal look so fabulous aren't really necessary. But they are fun. You may never have been much for fancy meals before you had baby, but now is the time to change. Children truly appreciate the way the food looks on their plate, and letting them do the "decorating" exposes them to new tastes and gives you critical time to finish up the meal.

How to do it: Consider letting your child put the following finishing touches on your family meals.

> *Special sprinkles:* Children may not want a pinch of dried parsley scattered over their meal, but they'll love sprinkling it over yours. And if you "ooh" and "ahh" over it enough on your meal, who knows? Maybe they'll add it to their own meal next time. Grated parmesan, sprinkles of paprika, or tiny cuttings of chives are other fun and fairly innocuous touches even to picky eaters. And every child will leap at the chance to add colored sugar sprinkles to the ice cream, pudding, cupcake, pancake, French toast, or waffle.

A little squeeze: Put jelly or peanut butter, tomato sauce, ketchup, salad dressing, or sour cream in a small squeeze bottle or cake-decorating bag and let your child squeeze designs, as appropriate, on meals. Don't put more of this in the bag or bottle than you want on your food—your child will certainly keep squeezing until it is empty.

Go for the garnish: While you try to finish preparing the meal, quickly set out a bowl each of mushrooms, baby carrots, cherry tomatoes, and single small pieces of lettuce, and tell your two-year-old to put one of each on every plate. This will take just long enough to let you finish preparing the main meal, and the garnish can serve as the salad you may not have had time to make yourself.

WRAP IT UP

Why not add baked potatoes to the menu?

Suggested Ages: Two years and up

Your Child's Special Skills and Interests: Highly developed motor skills, not putting things in mouth

Preparation Time: 5 minutes

Messiness Quotient: Low

The Sibling Factor: See Older-Child Variations below.

Materials: Potatoes, foil, pan filled with water, towel, toothbrush

Why to try it: As you read the directions in the cookbook, your toddler calmly folds and wraps potatoes, letting you concentrate on just when to add the next ingredient.

How to do it: First, let your child scrub (or finish scrubbing) the potatoes with a toothbrush in a pan filled with water. Give her a towel to set the wet potatoes on and another to dry each potato after it's been cleaned. Then, give your child small sheets of foil, showing her how to wrap the first potato and then letting her take over the process.

Older-Child Variations: Skip the potato part: Just give your two- or three-year-olds (well beyond the stage of putting things in their mouth) a piece of foil to play with. Let them fold, scrunch, and rip it—and roll it into balls to play games with.

BE A LITTLE CUT-UP

Safe "cutting" exercises for grown-up-feeling little guys.

Suggested Ages: Two and a half years and up

Your Child's Special Skills and Interests: Good hand-eye coordination, interested in cooking

Preparation Time: 5 minutes

Messiness Quotient: Medium to high

Materials: Plastic knife or butter knife

The Sibling Factor: Because this requires such close supervision, it's best to attempt it with just one child.

Commonsense Caution: Always keep all knives well out of reach of young children, and emphasize knife safety whenever you cut in front of them. Children should not use any knives without supervision.

Why to try it: This activity makes your child feel grown-up and capable of cutting like the big folks do—even if the knife is dull and the food is soft.

How to do it: As you cook, keep an eye out for ingredients that your child can practice cutting—a skill she's probably begging you to try. These should be items that can be sliced or cut with a butter knife: avocado, rindless watermelon, banana, or butter, for instance. Don't be limited by things that you *need* to have cut. If you are baking, you can even pack flour into a measuring cup, turn it upside down in the shallow bowl you'll be using, and let your child cut up the flour before you use it. Similarly, cutting packed cooked rice, pancakes, or white bread is a great kitchen exercise for a toddler. Once she's mastered the butter knife, graduate her to a serrated plastic table knife. And be sure to watch her closely when she uses either of these knives: Even a plastic table knife can cut skin. You'll also want to take the time when you use "safe" knives to re-emphasize that she should never use other, sharper knives in the kitchen by herself—or any knife if you aren't present.

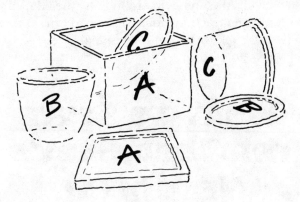

FIND THE RIGHT LID

This irritating task for you is fun and games for your child.

Suggested Ages: Three years and up

Your Child's Special Skills and Interests: Sorting, matching

Preparation Time: 15 minutes

Messiness Quotient: Negative—this project helps you straighten things out.

Materials: Permanent markers, plastic containers and lids

Why to try it: Matching and sorting are early mathematical skills; fitting lids and bottoms together helps teach shapes and increases fine motor skills.

How to do it: To help your child, and everyone in the house, better match the elusive lid to the corresponding container, take a few minutes to pair your plastic lids and containers up, and then draw matching letters, numbers, shapes, or designs on the lids and bottoms with a permanent marker. This will help everyone in the house find right away the lid he or she is looking for, while teaching your child (who can do this exercise while you cook) shapes, numbers, and letters.

WHAT TO SERVE FOR YOUR BABY'S NEXT MEAL

HAVE A THEME MEAL

Plan a meal according to shape, size, and color.

Suggested Ages: One year and up

Your Child's Special Skills and Interests: Learning shapes, colors, sizes, and textures

Preparation Time: Ongoing

Messiness Quotient: None

Materials: Food, melon baller, cookie cutters

Why to try it: Give your meal-planning creativity a boost and feed your child's brain and stomach at the same time by occasionally planning a meal according to food groups and shapes, colors, sizes, and so forth.

How to do it: First, decide on your theme. An orange meal, for example, might include macaroni and cheese, cantaloupe, carrots, or sweet-potato slices and orange juice; a pink meal could include the equally nutritious and kid-friendly combination of ham, watermelon, cranberry juice, and strawberries. Think your baby won't eat green? For St. Patrick's day try peas, avocado, and kiwi for an afternoon snack. Along with colors, babies are also into shapes and, at around one year, balls. So make a meal that rolls: blueberries, melon balls, peas, and cheese balls made out of processed cheese and cracker crumbs. A mini-meal is another winner. Tiny things have great appeal to kids, starting at around 18 months of age. Serve up mini-versions of muffins (you can buy mini-muffin pans) doughnuts, waffles, or pancakes, mini-size pizzas or hamburgers, and even mini-sandwiches (sandwiches cut into quarters). Serve the food on a tiny plate (such as a white plastic container lid, flipped upside down) with a tiny cup and mini-cutlery (raid your child's toy closet for these). As your child gets closer to preschool age, you can also try "math" meals: Give your child two apple slices, two cookies, two carrots, two pieces of sandwich, or give him one of one item, two of another, three of another, and so on. Alphabet cookie cutters, available through gourmet-cooking catalogs, are handy for reinforcing letter learning. Use them to cut letters in bread and cheese and even slices of watermelon.

BE A BIG DIPPER

Your little dipper's inventiveness might surprise you both.

Suggested Ages: 18 months and up

Your Child's Special Skills and Interests:
Enjoys feeding herself

Preparation Time: 10 to 15 minutes

Messiness Quotient: High

Materials: Paper plates or bowls, plastic forks or flat rounded-tip
toothpicks, dipping items (see below)

> **Commonsense Caution:** Check your pediatri-
> cian's recommendations for when to introduce
> milk products, nuts, and various fruits and vege-
> tables before adding them to the dipping table.
> Peanut butter is a great dip but, because of the
> potential for allergic reactions, is generally not
> recommended until a child is at least three. Check
> with your pediatrician first.

Why to try it: A little dip of "special sauce" is often all your
child needs to eat vegetables, fresh fruits, and more.

How to do it: Set out a selection of different dips in small
cups or bowls and a number of items cut into kid-size bites for
dipping, as well as a few dried items for a final dip of "sprinkles." Show your child how to dip with a fork first; at around
two or so let her try using a flat rounded toothpick to dip as
well. Then try not to be judgmental when your child grabs a
fork, spears an apple, then dips it in salsa and happily eats it.

Consider putting the following items out at your child's dipping bar:

TO DIP	DIP	FINAL DIP
Steamed asparagus	Salad dressing	Grated parmesan
Graham crackers	Apple Sauce	Cinnamon sugar
Bread sticks	Pizza sauce	Grated mozzarella
Strawberries	Sour cream	Brown sugar
Apple slices	Cream cheese	Dried hot-chocolate mix
Pretzel sticks	Melted, cooled cheese	
Whole-grain bread	Yogurt	Soft raisins
String-cheese sticks	Mild salsa	Graham-cracker crumbs
Cooked rigatoni		Bread crumbs
Mini-pancackes or waffles		

Pretend-Play Dipping Variation: Turn breadsticks into fishing rods, cream cheese or peanut butter into bait, and "go fish" for animal crackers. Simply show your child how to dip the "rods" into a container of cream cheese or peanut butter (or anything else sticky you can think of), and then dip them in the bowl of crackers. Lift the rods up and eat your catch!

ENJOY A TODDLER TEA

Take a seat and sit on the floor.

Suggested Ages: 18 months to three years

Your Child's Special Skills and Interests: Eating on own, talking well

Preparation Time: 15 to 20 minutes

Messiness Quotient: Medium

Materials: Tea set, blanket, cloth napkins, cookie cutters

Why to try it: A change of scene and attitude can rev up little appetites and inspire new manners. And tea-time menus are generally made as if for toddlers: Foods served in bite-size portions, on separate plates, with no icky sauces. If you serve a mix of sweet and savory items, tea can easily replace a lunch or dinner. And teas allow eating over a longish period of time, perfect for the grazing habits so typical of toddlers.

How to do it: Turn lunch or dinner into an event by calling it tea, inviting over a friend or two (of yours or your child's) and throwing a pretty blanket on the kitchen floor. Let everyone sit around the blanket as you serve tea and tea-time foods: crackers topped with cheese, ham, or turkey slices cut into hearts and stars with cookie cutters; thin slices of melon and mini–pumpkin muffins; a bowl of berries; a plate of carrots, celery, and pickles; a few hard-boiled eggs; and a plate of sweets, of course. As for the beverage itself: Choose what is technically called an infusion and is more commonly referred to as an herbal tea; fruit flavors will be most popular. Be sure to serve it with milk and sugar—stirring and passing are critical elements to this party. And set a formal mood: Politely ask for everything to be passed to you (even when you could reach it yourself) and cater to the other adults as well as to the children in this way. You'll notice that even very young children will quickly try to follow suit. When the tea is over, simply remove the dishes and throw your blanket (crumbs and all) into the wash.

GO INTO THE DEEP FREEZE

Why heat it up when you can serve it cold?

Suggested Ages: 18 months and up

Your Child's Special Skills and Interests: Eating on own

Preparation Time: Variable

Messiness Quotient: Low—until stuff starts melting

Materials: Popsicle forms

Why to try it: Cold food feels good on sore gums and cools down active toddlers. Plus, serving things cold saves you the heat-it-up-then-wait-till-it-cools step.

How to do it: Sometimes a change in temperature is all your child needs to find new interest in an old food. For example:

Breakfast Pops: Let your child help you mix up a fruit smoothie in the blender (equal parts banana, yogurt, orange juice, frozen fruit, soft tofu) and then freeze it in a Popsicle mold. Serve the "pops" with a frozen waffle, and you will have covered three food groups—fruit, bread, and dairy—in an out-of-the-freezer meal.

Frozen Yogurt Sandwich: Sandwich several spoonfuls of yogurt and a few pieces of frozen fruit in between two graham crackers, wrap everything in aluminum foil, and freeze it—for a frozen treat that's healthy too.

Frozen Fruit: Peel and freeze bananas and clean, stemless strawberries on sheets of wax paper, and then serve them with chocolate sauce for a dessert that is at least half-way healthy.

SHAKE IT UP, BABY

Dance for your dessert with these fun baby recipes.

Suggested Ages: 18 months to three years

Your Child's Special Skills and Interests: Dancing and wild,
energetic movement

Preparation Time: 10 minutes (20 minutes for making butter)

Messiness Quotient: Medium to high—especially if the bag
comes open

Materials: Self-sealing gallon- and half-gallon-size plastic bags,
dessert items (see below)

Why to try it: Your child will love burning off extra energy
and actually making something good to eat at the same time.

How to do it: Explain to your child that she is going to trans-
form simple food like sliced bananas into a delectable
cinnamon-raisin-banana dessert by shaking up banana slices
in a plastic bag filled with several spoonfuls of cinnamon-sugar
and a few soft raisins. All she has to do is drop in the bananas,
seal up the bag, and then dance around until they are coated.
Other possible combinations:

Banana slices coated with dried sweetened hot-
chocolate mix.

Apple slices coated with cinnamon-sugar or grated par-
mesan cheese.

Strawberries coated with powdered sugar.

Lightly buttered toast squares coated with grated par-
mesan cheese.

Old-fashioned Variation: If you have a young butter lover or a hyper two-year-old, have him shake up the butter for dinner. Put a container of heavy cream in a plastic jar with a very secure lid. Take turns shaking it for 20 minutes or so, and watch what happens: It will get thicker and thicker until you can spread it—it's butter!

MAKE ART FOR DESSERT

Five edible finger paints to try.

Suggested Ages: 18 months and up

Your Child's Special Skills and Interests: Beginning
to finger-paint

Preparation Time: 15 minutes

Messiness Quotient: Very high

Materials: Dry flavored gelatin, spray bottle; whipped cream,
food coloring; sweetened condensed milk, food coloring; waxed
paper, tape

Why to try it: Try these activities to provide an exciting finale for your next lunch. The messes of art and eating are combined for efficient cleanup.

How to do it: Tape one end of a roll of waxed paper to your work surface, letting the other end drape down over the side. As your child paints on the paper, you can rip off the taped end and toss the used section, then pull up another piece to work on. If the weather is warm, you might consider doing this activity outside; otherwise, be sure to have plenty of towels underneath the table, baby stripped down to his diaper, and a bath waiting. (You won't want to be wearing nice clothes either, since you'll have to carry messy baby to clean up.) Now let baby try finger painting with the following mixtures:

Flavored gelatin and water: Sprinkle dry gelatin on the waxed paper, then spray or drip the surface lightly with water and let your child run her fingers through the mix to make designs with it. You can also try this activity with instant pudding and water.

Whipped cream and food coloring: Spray whipped cream on the paper, then add food coloring and let baby mix the two substances together. Teach her about colors by combining colors to see what new ones can be made.

Sweetened condensed milk and food coloring: Put several tablespoons of condensed milk on the waxed surface, then add food coloring and let baby mix everything together, licking her fingers as she chooses.

Applesauce and cinnamon-sugar: Spoon applesauce on the paper, then let baby shake on a cinnamon-sugar mixture out of a container. Watch as the cinnamon turns the applesauce brown and tasty.

Yogurt and dried gelatin: Spoon out plain or vanilla yogurt, then let baby shake on different colors of dried gelatin (sugar-free or regular) to change the color and texture.

OR: MAKE DESSERT INTO ART

String the meal along with these activities.

Suggested Ages: Two years and up

Your Child's Special Skills and Interests: Developing fine motor skills adequate for stringing large beads

Preparation Time: 5 minutes

Messiness Quotient: Medium

Materials: Bag of string licorice, colored and shaped cereal,
small pretzels or doughnuts or any other food or
candy with a hole in the middle

Why to try it: This activity results in a sweet treat, keeping
everyone busy and happy.

How to do it: Cut up lengths of string licorice, then show
your child how to string candy, doughnuts, or cereal to make
a necklace. (Be sure to knot the end so that all the necklace
goodies don't slide off.) Once he's completed his creation,
let him wear it around the house until he gets too hungry to
resist it.

Variations: You can also string homemade cookies on licorice. Simply use a bamboo skewer to carve out a hole in the
cookies right after they have been baked and are cooling.

MAKE PEEK-A-BOO FOOD

Treats with a surprise inside.

Suggested Ages: Two years and up

Your Child's Special Skills and Interests: Notices and enjoys the
little differences that make "surprises"

Preparation Time: 15 minutes

Messiness Quotient: Medium to high

Materials: Melon baller or set of measuring teaspoons,
vegetables and fruits (see below)

Why to try it: It's a simple way to stuff nutrition and flavor in a surprise treat your child will love to eat.

How to do it: Turn vegetables and fruits into surprise packages by hollowing out their insides with a teaspoon, replacing them with fun fillings, and then putting the halves back together again. Then, when you are ready, be sure to pull them apart to show the insides with all the pizzazz of a magic show: Surprise!

Some Possibilities:

Strawberries: Slice them vertically and fill with flavored cream cheese, chocolate spread, or even fresh blueberries.

Cherry tomatoes: Slice them horizontally and fill them with plain or flavored cream cheese or a processed cheese spread.

Apples: Core them and then fill the insides with peanut butter, chocolate spread, or cinnamon-sugar and small marshmallows.

Bananas: Fold back a single peel. Now make a vertical slit down the flesh of the banana and fill the space with peanut butter and a few small chocolate chips. Replace the peel, and hand the banana to your toddler for peeling and eating.

Baked surprises: Add cheese, jam, or chocolate to the inside of muffins or biscuits. Drop just half the batter, add a teaspoon or chunk of the surprise ingredient, cover it with the remaining batter, and bake.

HAVE YOUR ALPHABET AND EAT IT, TOO

A sweet lesson your child won't forget.

Suggested Ages: Two years and up

Your Child's Special Skills and Interests: Learning shapes,
numbers, or letters

Preparation Time: 10 minutes

Messiness Quotient: None

Materials: Flat candy wafers (such as Necco), toothpicks,
food coloring

Why to try it: This project turns dessert into real fun and
games.

How to do it: Dip a toothpick into one of your vials of food
coloring, and use it to draw one shape, letter, or number on
each of your candy wafers. Put them out on the table and challenge your child to eat "his letter" and "his number" or to
match candy wafers with the same letters together. Each time
he succeeds at your challenge, he gets to eat his reward.

Non-Sugar Variation: Write numbers and letters with a can of squeeze cheese on plain crackers and play the same mix-and-match game as an appetizer rather than as dessert.

MAKE A CRACKER QUILT

Try geometry you eat for a snack.

Suggested Ages: Two years and up

Your Child's Special Skills and Interests: Learning shapes

Preparation Time: 5 minutes

Messiness Quotient: Medium

Materials: Crackers shaped like circles, triangles, and rectangles

Why to try it: Learning shapes is a pre-reading skill; seeing how shapes are put together is early geometry. And it's fun, too.

How to do it: Give your child a flat surface—such as a tray or clean tabletop—and a handful of crackers of various shapes. Before she starts snacking, show your child how to arrange the crackers in quilt-like patterns. Put a circle cracker in the center and place triangles around the edge for a star or flower pattern, or arrange squares to form a checkerboard, a house, a hop-scotch grid, or any number of designs.

Full-Meal Variation: You can also try this exercise with a homemade pizza: Cut slices of mozzarella cheese into various shapes, and then lay them out in designs on top of a tomato-sauce-covered pizza to create a pizza-quilt.

Color Your Cuisine

When you want your child to eat more than white bread.

Suggested Ages: Two years and up

Your Child's Special Skills and Interests: Painting, colors

Preparation Time: 10 minutes

Messiness Quotient: High

Materials: Clean milk jug lid or other lids, diluted food colorings (two drops diluted by two drops of water), clean paintbrushes, bagels cut in half, slices of cantaloupe or apple, or other flat, paintable food

Why to try it: Color adds an extra dimension to your child's culinary experience.

How to do it: Fill the lids with diluted food colorings and set them on a covered surface. Now let your child color the circle of his bagel or the side of his cantaloupe or apple. When he's finished with the creation, he can pop it in his mouth.

Natural Dye Variation: For a natural (but staining) food dye, use the drippings from frozen blueberries, strawberries, or raspberries, or a teaspoon of melted frozen juice concentrate.

Chapter Three

~~~~~~~~

NAP TIMES

Planning and Projects, Just for Parents

Nap time. Most parents of babies can't imagine life without it. And they shouldn't. Naps should be a regular part of your daily life with baby during the first three years, both for baby's physical and emotional growth and for a parent's sanity and health. While baby naps, parents are able to have at least a few hours of rest time during each day for napping themselves, for returning phone calls, or for simply filing their nails. How each parent uses these precious moments is a personal decision. But because these hours are so limited, they hold a special status for many parents, who want to use them as effectively as possible. Most of the time, these hours should or must be devoted to a parent's personal, business, or household needs. But nap time can also sometimes be used for the fun parenting projects we may want to do but can't find a moment for during the busier hours when baby is up. Nap time ties us down to the house and so can offer the opportunity to try projects to prepare us for baby's waking hours, to connect baby to distant family, and to create souvenirs of these fast-moving years that—like nap times—are over too quickly.

WHAT TO DO DURING BABY'S NAP TIME

KEEP AN INFORMAL PARENTING JOURNAL

Materials: Blank book, pen or pencil

Why to try it: To preserve your thoughts on your child and your own parenting experience.

How to do it: The last thing you need in your life is more to do. Still, there are probably details of your life as a parent, and your baby's life as a baby, that you'd like to be able to remember when your child grows up and starts asking questions, and recording memorable times will take some time and effort. Since your child won't be able to remember these times—and you probably won't be able to, either—a journal, kept only as often as you can get to it, can help. Before you start a baby journal, remind yourself not to be overly ambitious. Sometimes you'll only be able to get to the journal once every other nap, once a week, or maybe even twice a month. But if you make a habit of sitting down with your journal for just a few minutes right after your child lies down for his nap—in those uncertain first few minutes when you hesitate to take on anything more ambitious—you might just end up with a fairly complete record of these years.

Less Intimidating Variation for Non-writers: Keep notes about what baby is doing in your regular personal calendar or datebook. If you have made a life change (such as from working to staying at home) keeping your calendar full of these notes will help you see how much you and baby are still getting done at home, even if you don't have any meetings or appointments to pencil in.

CREATE A SCRAPBOOK FOR BABY OF FAMILY AND FRIENDS

Materials: Blank archival-quality scrapbook, preferably with plastic sheet protectors on the pages; archival tape, glue or photo corners, archival-quality pen, current photographs of family and friends

Why to try it: Babies love to look at photographs. A photo album is a great way for you to prepare baby for visiting friends and family.

How to do it: Group together favorite photos of the important people in your life in a special book for baby, preferably with protective plastic pages to protect it from baby's loving mitts. Devote a page or two to each family member or friend, picking photos that clearly show faces, homes, and other important details about the person. If you'd like, you might even write down his or her name in large letters so you can point it out to your child, as well as something about your relationship to the person—and, by extension—the relationship of the person to your baby. Grouping photos of an individual together allows baby to look at each person in detail without confusion.

TURN YOUR FAMILY AND FRIENDS INTO KITCHEN MAGNETS

Materials: Photographs, sharp scissors, sheets of self-adhesive magnets (available at most photo and craft shops for about a dollar for two 4- by 6-inch sheets)

Why to try it: These kitchen magnets bring family and friends to life for baby, and keep your child occupied and in sight at the refrigerator door while you cook or talk on the phone.

How to do it: Make a point of taking photographs of family and friends at your next big get-together. Baby's first Christ-

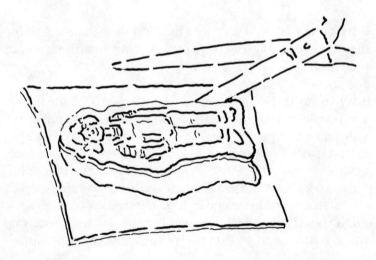

mas, Hanukkah, Kwanzaa, birthday, or baptism should provide particularly good opportunities. For optimal effect, make sure the photos are shot relatively close up and show the subject's entire body from head to toe. Loosely cut around the person in the photo, without cutting into the image, then place the photo on the adhesive part of the magnet. Now cut closely around the image and magnet to make a paper-doll-like cutout of the subject. Ultimately, group a whole gang together on the refrigerator.

Non-Metal-Refrigerator Variation: If you don't have a metal-covered refrigerator, create another magnet play area in your kitchen by framing a large piece of tin (available at lumberyards) with wood strips and nailing or hanging the whole apparatus on a blank kitchen wall.

KEEP FRIENDS UP-TO-DATE WITH BABY

Materials: Envelopes, address book, stamps, photographs

Why to try it: So you'll never be nagged about sending a photograph of baby again.

How to do it: Make a list of your closest friends and relatives, and address and stamp a dozen envelopes to each person. Always ask for doubles when you have your photographs processed. Put one set of photos aside for baby's scrapbook (to be filled during another nap) and use the other set to drop one picture each into your waiting envelopes. Since the addressing is already done, you can send the photos out promptly and easily. This will only take a few minutes, which is good, since if it isn't nap time, a few minutes is usually all the time you have.

DEVELOP A FAMILY ARCHIVE

Materials: Three very sturdy shoe or boot boxes with lids or store-bought photo boxes, peel-on labels, archival-quality pens, ribbons, steel fireproof safety box

Why to try it: The longer you wait to develop a system for storing family memories, the more likely it will be that the most memorable thing your child will inherit is a mess of boxes.

How to do it: Start by labeling your cardboard boxes on the outside with the child's name and the year. Make boxes for the first three years at once, so you'll have a system in place as baby grows. To make things easier, start and end your box's calendar year with baby's birthday each year. This consistent date—which is already devoted to your child anyway—is the perfect time to record the developmental highlights of the year, growth statistics, hand- and footprints, and other personal details about your child. Write these statistics and information on a piece of paper glued inside the lid. For this annual information sheet, consider going beyond just physical or developmental growth each year. Write down a few meaningful details or anecdotes about what baby was like personally as well—this will mean more to your child than when he first ate with a spoon. You can tie special birthday cards together with ribbon and put them in the box, and as baby begins to explore his artistic side, you can add several favorite pieces of art each year as well. Try to limit yourself to the size of the one box you have—remember, you'll have well over a dozen of these boxes by the time your child is grown, so more than one per year will become a lot to store. Keep this in mind and be selective—and consistent. Try to put the same type of information and memorabilia in each box every year so your child will ultimately have a continuing record of the same sorts of things through the years. You can also use these boxes to store photographs throughout the year, pulling them out to put in albums during nap times or during one big album session right before baby's birthday. In the large locked, fireproof box, put the negatives of your photographs and copies of your videotapes. If possible, store these outside of your home. That way, if your home is destroyed in a fire, flood, or other natural disaster, you'll still have copies of these irreplaceable memories to pass on to your child.

MAKE TOYS FOR BABY

Materials

Shape Sorter: shoebox, coffee can or large plastic container; tapes, extra lids

Felt Boards: felt, cardboard, scissors, glue

Chalk Box: chalkboard paint, cigar box, Velcro tabs

Personalized Magnets: self-adhesive magnet sheets and small cookie sheet

Why to try it: Homemade toys are not only less expensive, they can also reflect your child's current tastes better than anything you can buy at the store.

How to do it:

Shape Sorter: Six months and up. Cut one mail-box-like hole or several small holes in the top of a shoebox, in the lid of a large coffee can, or in the side of a clear large plastic container with a lid and large enough for you to reach your hand inside. Now collect old lids (such as those from the top of juice cans) that are too large to be ingested. Your child can drop the lids in the box or can and then retrieve them by taking off the container's lid, or drop them in the plastic jar or coffee can and shake them around until you get them out. In either case, it's a free toy that you'll both love.

Felt Boards: One year and up. For around five dollars or less, you can make a take-it-along felt board for your child. Simply cut a square or circle out of heavy cardboard, and glue a sheet or two of felt onto the surface. Using cookie cutters or magazine cutouts as patterns, cut out shapes, figures, letters, and more in colors that are your child's favorites of the moment. Store these in a self-sealing plastic bag taped to the back of the felt board. Feeling inept cutting out your own designs with scissors? You can also cut out photos or magazine pictures, glue them to sturdy cardboard, and put a felt strip on the back—they work on a felt board just like regular felt pieces but have more details.

Personalized Magnets: One year and up. Cut out pictures of your baby's favorite foods, animals, flowers, and so forth, and place them on the adhesive side of self-adhesive magnet sheets. Cut carefully around the outline to make personalized magnets for baby. Present them to him after his nap on a small metal cookie sheet where he can stick and re-stick them.

Chalkboard Boxes: 18 months and up. You can purchase slate or chalkboard paint at most paint stores. Spray or paint it on the lid of a sturdy cardboard box (cigar-box-like varieties are available at craft stores, and real cigar boxes are available at cigar shops, naturally) and use a self-adhesive Velcro tab as a closure. In one afternoon, you can make a chalkboard and chalk storage container perfect for at-home or on the road use.

MAKE OLD TOYS NEW AGAIN

Materials: None

Why to try it: To call fresh attention to old toys.

How to do it: Every few weeks or so as you pick up toys from the morning's activities while your child is napping, make a point of re-arranging their locations when you put them back. Put new books in the easy-to-reach section of the bookshelf. Take toys from the bedroom and put them in the living room toy baskets. Put other toys in unexpected locations: a basket of blocks in the background; an arrangement of racing cars or tea sets on an open shelf in the kitchen; a set of crayons on your child's favorite step. You might even make a regular habit of removing some toys from your child's reach, and then re-presenting them at another time. When your child awakes from her naps, she'll see a whole new world of playtime choices.

SORT YOUR TRASH FOR TOYS

Materials: Laundry basket or large sturdy waste can or
cardboard box

Why to try it: If you need an extra incentive for sorting out your cabinets, closets, and drawers during nap times, consider the treasures that might await you and your child in these cluttered recesses.

How to do it: As you consolidate containers and clean up and organize your house, consider the following fun uses for commonly thrown-away objects. To keep them from overtaking your storage space, keep them corraled in a laundry basket or specially marked trash can, tossing or using them when they begin to overflow their confines.

Mailing tubes: Fill them with pebbles and tightly cap and secure both ends with tape, then give the constructions to your child to paint or decorate and use as rattles or "rain sticks."

Bubble wrap: Show your child how to paint the bubble-topped surface and then press it against paper to make beautiful snake-skin-like prints.

Dental floss containers: Pry out the metal floss dispenser with a screwdriver and give the empty container to your child as a fun little treasure box. You can even turn it into a necklace—use nails to make holes on each

side and then string it up with yarn. Small plastic candy containers are also useful for the same purposes.

Plastic yogurt containers, small glass jars, tea and coffee cans, oatmeal containers, tissue boxes, small jewelry boxes: You always need a selection of these for insect homes, paintbrush jars, homemade drum making, doll-house construction, and more.

Styrofoam packing forms: With all their nooks and crannies, these can easily become doll houses, horse corrals, or even color-marker or crayon holders, if you find one that has numerous vertical holes just that size. You can also use one like a kind of maze, rolling a ball (or marble, for a non-oral child) around inside.

Lids: Stack them, sort them, roll them. You can change their looks with a layer of contact paper, use them in crafts projects as eyes, and turn them into game pieces or pretend pocket change.

BE READY FOR AFTER-NAP CRANKINESS

Materials: None

Why to try it: To ease the sometimes difficult and cranky transition from napping to wakefulness.

How to do it: Sometimes nothing will help bring your baby back to the world of the happily conscious. But setting up the following activities while your baby or toddler sleeps might help either immediately or after her irritability wears off.

Show her something new. As you carry baby from her crib, have an exciting destination: A fresh bouquet of flowers. A neat rock. A photo album you just finished adding pictures to. Check out the latest happenings with the fish, the mailman, and the dog.

Give him a project. Before baby wakes, lay out all the ingredients for a recipe or a craft or cleaning project, keeping in mind just what steps will be right for baby to try himself or which he will enjoy watching. When he wakes up, bring him to the project immediately and show him the first step.

Try something soothing. After-nap is sometimes as good a time to read books as before nap. Have a pile of books, a snack, and a cozy blanket handy for wake-up reading sessions. Listening to soft music and doing a puzzle or writing or drawing in a journal are also calming wake-up activities.

Have a snack ready. Have a refreshing treat ready when your baby awakes: a smoothie, fresh fruit or vegetables, graham crackers and milk. These can be just what your child needs to make the transition to wakefulness in some semblance of good humor.

MAKE NOTES

Materials: Paper and pen or pencil

Why to try it: Many parents report a sudden brain loss when they are in the middle of caring for their children. Standing amid a sea of toys and paper and paints, looking at their child's longing, expectant face, they can't remember what they were going to do.

How to do it: Teachers make lesson plans, why shouldn't you? Making a list of games or activities or outings to try with your child after the nap, as well as a list of any personal goals you can work on while caring for your child, will keep you on track when your child wakes up in a fit and you don't know what to do. Being able to cross things off a list and see what you have accomplished will make you feel productive and successful and save you from those momentary memory lapses that can make your life feel somewhat out of control.

Chapter Four

~~~~~~~~~

AFTERNOONS

Quick and Easy Activities for You and Your Baby

You've played and cleaned up and played and cleaned up and been patient all day. Or perhaps you've been hard at work outside the home. You may be about to be relieved by a spouse, or you may be on your own for the twelfth hour in a row. In any case, it is likely that by this hour, your top priority (you) is a little bit more self-centered than your young child—who considers himself the center of the universe—would like. Your demands are not unreasonable, by adult standards anyway. You want to eat, cook dinner, read the mail, or return a phone call. But there is nothing like needing just a moment to yourself to inspire your young child to decide that he desperately needs you. Right now.

The main thing your child wants—in addition to you, of course—is the knowledge that you are still paying attention and haven't forgotten her entirely in your rush toward a little personal productivity. Being able to pull out several of the low-prep, low-mess, minimal-supervision activities described in this chapter will keep everyone happy. Be sure to milk each activity for all it is worth before moving on to another. This will let your child fully explore the possibilities of each thing you do and give you some time to get other chores done.

Of course, if you've been gone all day, launching into activities that somewhat free you from your child won't always work right away. If your child isn't going along with doing anything you suggest, consider sitting down beside him to talk, read, or cuddle quietly for a few minutes before beginning your projects and setting him up with his own activities. A small investment in reconnecting with your child before starting something new can make all the difference in the afternoon's success for both you and him.

A positive attitude is also particularly crucial in the late afternoon. In a recent study kids were asked what they most wanted from their parents. Researchers suspected that they would want more time with Mom and Dad, but what they actually said was that they wanted their parents to be less stressed—a powerful statement about how your attitudes affect your children.

And if you can't be cheery in the face of chores and kids and phone and job, consider being silly instead. Silliness can be a serious tool when you are fighting battles over diaper changes or are facing the prospect of chasing a toddler who won't put down the bowl of chocolate sauce or come back within your reach. Using a silly voice, pretend to be the contents of the diaper, desperately wanting to get out of the diaper trap, or fall down on the floor and begin singing a melodramatic tune about the chocolate sauce you loved and lost. Sudden actions, funny faces, weird voices, out-of-character reactions: All of these should be in the silly parents' repertoire, ready to be pulled out to startle or humor your child out of an imminent stand-off of the wills (and, not incidentally, probably help your child develop a sense of humor as well). Other silly things you can try to amuse or distract a baby or toddler include:

SILLY SOLUTIONS TO AFTERNOON CRANKINESS

Whisper unexpectedly

Put on sunglasses or a funny hat

Whistle

Dance

Howl at the moon

Fall down

Put underwear on your head

Brush the doll's or stuffed animal's teeth with an electric toothbrush

Crawl, hop, twirl, or skip

Talk to inanimate objects

Sing (be sure to insert baby's name in lyrics)

Maniacal laughter or giggling

Use your hands as talking puppets

Stick your fingers in your ear

Wear shoes on your hands

WHAT TO DO THIS AFTERNOON

WATCH THE FAN GO ROUND AND ROUND

Alternatives for families without ceiling fans.

Suggested Ages: Birth to six months

Your Child's Special Skills and Interests: None

Preparation Time: 10 minutes

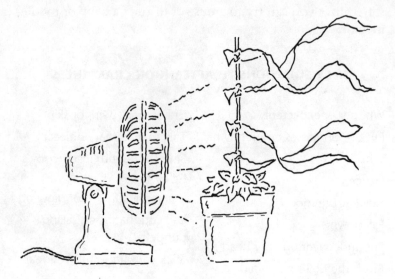

Messiness Quotient: Low

Materials: Floor or tabletop fan, ribbons

Commonsense caution: Don't put any fans within baby's reach from their seats—or on the floor at all if baby can crawl.

Why to try it: Ceiling fans have saved the sanity of many parents of infants. Pop a baby underneath the mesmerizing circular motion of a fan and presto: instant trance.

How to do it: Tie ribbons or colorful crepe paper to a many-branched stick or a wooden ruler, and put the stick into the soil of a planter filled with rocks or soil. Now put your ribbon plant in front of a floor fan and within sight of baby, who can watch the ribbons flutter and move in the wind. At night, move the fan and ribbon plant in front of a light so that baby can watch the changing shadows on the wall.

Other Variations: Hang a wind chime in the wind pattern of a rotating fan and let it move and tinkle in the wind. In addition to this, consider creating indoor wind sculptures by hanging objects in front of a fan—and well out of reach of a baby: Tie feathers to a string and hang them from a stick. Anchor Mylar balloons with tape to a wall (regular latex balloons, when popped, are a severe choking hazard). Tie tinsel to the branches of a potted plant, or stick pinwheels in the soil where the fan can make them blow around and around.

Take It Outside

A change of scene is what you need.

Suggested Ages: Birth and up

Your Child's Special Skills and Interests: None

Preparation Time: None

Messiness Quotient: Less than when inside

Materials: Variable

Why to try it: If you've been inside most of the day working and the weather is warm, the best way to lift and keep spirits up is to move everything outside. It's simpler than you think.

How to do it: Think of your evening out as a kind of modified camping trip and keep everything simple. Move what you need outside at the start and then cook on the grill, eat your meal—even do the bath and bedtime ritual—under open skies. Rain, of course, has a way of ruining these plans, but there are ways around it, especially if you have a garage. Move the cars out, open up the garage door, and ride bikes, do crafts, even have a picnic in a well-swept blanket-covered corner while you watch the rain fall outside. Doesn't the rain smell good?

Eating: Move the high chair outside and leave cleaning up to the birds, the dog, or the hose. If your child is out of the high chair, eat outside anyway, on a blanket or at a table.

Bathe al fresco: Fill the outdoor wading pool with warm water, or move the baby tub outside. Splashing is now acceptable.

Cuddle Time: Watch the sunset and read the first book of the night in a pile of pillows and blankets piled up outside. After a while in the fresh air, bedtime will be easy.

Crafts: Paint splatters? Who cares, when you have a hose ready to wash it all away?

BOUNCE AND SPIN

You get to sit down, baby gets to move.

Suggested Ages: Birth to nine months

Your Child's Special Skills and Interests: None

Preparation Time: None

Messiness Quotient: None

Materials: Swivel chair, large-fit ball or bouncy cushion

Commonsense Caution: Be sure to rock or bounce your baby very gently, always supporting his head and neck.

Why to try it: Movement is calming for some babies who are cranky in the afternoon, especially a gentle bounce or rocking side-to-side motion.

How to do it: Sit on a fit ball or other large ball and, with your baby securely in your grasp, gently bounce up and down, being careful to keep your feet stable on the ground. A swivel office chair is also a great alternative to the up-and-down motion of a rocking chair—and you can relax as you swing back and forth with baby in your lap.

TRY NATURAL ENTERTAINMENT

Soothing home experiences with natural baby appeal.

Suggested ages: Birth and up

Your Child's Special Skills and Interests: None

Preparation Time: Ongoing

Messiness Quotient: None

Materials: Bird feeders, wind socks, wind chimes,
light catchers

Why to try it: These natural entertainers take over the job of amusing baby with very little effort from you.

How to do it: If you've thought a wind sock or wind chime was a luxury you didn't need, now is the time to reconsider. These simple nature-based pleasures are great distractions for babies, who find the unpredictable movements of wind, light, and birds fascinating. Consider adding the following natural entertainers to your home.

Rainbow prism/Light catchers: Hung in a light window, these shimmering beauties catch baby's attention on their own. But when hit with direct sunlight, they also create rainbows and patterns all around the room. Hang several in baby's room and in other rooms where you spend a lot of time. *Commonsense Caution: Be sure to keep the strings hanging these light catchers well out of baby's reach.*

Wind sock, wind chime, or wind sculpture: Hung near a window low enough for baby to see out of, wind toys are fabulous infant toy investments. And you may find you come to enjoy watching them as well. If you live in an apartment where hanging things outside is difficult, hang your wind toys inside, and open the window for a gentle breeze.

Bird feeders: The sudden, quick movements of birds, as well as the drama of a flock coming to your feeder, make birds endlessly amusing. The bird feeders that attach right to the window offer baby a close-up view and work well for apartment dwellers, but a series of bird feeders stuck in the ground or hanging from a tree will provide you and baby with plenty of excitement too.

FIND SURPRISES IN JUNK

Finding playthings that come in the mail.

Suggested Ages: Six months and up

Your Child's Special Skills and Interests: Sitting up

Preparation Time: None

Messiness Quotient: None

Materials: Your mail

Why to try it: You need to sort the mail anyway, right?

How to do it: As you go through your mail, be on the lookout for coupon books, perfume samples, stickers, and more. Your junk mail is your baby's treasure. Let him smell coupon scratch-and-sniffs, lick stickers, flip through coupon books, and scratch off prize squares. If he is very young, keep your eye on him and your hand on the mail so he doesn't eat or mouth these junk-mail treasures.

Variations: Keep an eye out for samples while you are shopping. Paint chips, carpet samples, and wallpaper sample books are great toys for baby. Always ask at home improvement stores if they are retiring any of their samples or sample books and would be willing to give them to you. Another great free resource: Stock photography books. These are sometimes available through advertising agencies. The photos are arranged by category, making them wonderful books for babies, with pages of photos of happy people, couples, families, animals, trees, clouds, and so forth.

LOOK AT COOL STUFF

Make these quick, intriguing toys for an infant.

Suggested Ages: Six months and up

Your Child's Special Skills and Interests: Able to hold, shake, and roll an object

Preparation Time: 5 minutes

Messiness Quotient: None

Materials: Plastic jar with lid and opening diameter wider than baby's hand, brightly colored marbles, ¾-inch diameter plastic tubing (2 feet long), duct tape

> **Commonsense Caution:** If you put the lid on tightly and it is wider than your baby's hand, she should not be able to open the jar. However, for extra safety, ring the top with extra tape to seal the jar, and don't let baby play with it or the hula toy unsupervised.

Why to try it: Babies are endlessly amused by watching things roll.

How to do it: Put a marble or two in a plastic jar, put the lid on tightly, and hand it to baby. She will turn it upside down and over and around many times, watching the marbles roll round and round. If she can crawl, she might enjoy rolling the whole enterprise across the floor.

To make another roll-toy, slip two marbles inside a two-foot length of ¾-inch diameter plastic tubing, and tape the two ends together to make a small circle. Hand to baby and show her how moving the circle up or down makes the marbles roll faster and faster.

BOX UP YOUR BABY

Cardboard box fun for babies.

Suggested Ages: 9 to 18 months

Your Child's Special Skills and Interests: Sitting on own, crawling

Preparation Time: 15 minutes

Messiness Quotient: Medium to high, especially if the oatmeal spills

Materials: Cardboard box big enough to hold a sitting baby and a few toys comfortably, scissors, colored markers, uncooked oatmeal, cups, and spoons

Why to try it: Perhaps because most of their early life is spent in very tight quarters, babies find comfort in tiny places. Or maybe they just like a change of scene. In any case, a cardboard box also provides a place for them to practice filling and emptying, and even shape sorting.

How to do it:

Oatmeal Box. Pour an inch or two of uncooked oatmeal across the bottom of a cardboard box (be sure to tape down flaps and cover holes) for a simple indoor "sandbox." Now set your baby inside with plastic cups and spoons to dig and "pour" with. Of course, he'll try eating a little oatmeal (it's healthy) and may drop some over the side of the box, so set the box on top of a beach towel for easier cleanup indoors, or put it on the porch for no-hassle outdoor fun.

Big-Time Shape Sorter. Draw a number of shapes on the outside of a cardboard box, outlining them with a marker inside and out with wide bands of different colors. Then cut through them with a serrated knife. Young babies like to play Peek-a-boo through the holes; older babies will enjoy sending various objects like balls and blocks in and out of the openings. Develop or reinforce their knowledge of shapes and colors by identifying which hole—and which color—you are popping each object through.

DELIVER THE MAIL

A just-learning-to-walk activity for your child, while you read the mail.

Suggested Ages: 9 to 18 months

Your Child's Special Skills and Interests: Just learning to walk holding on

Preparation Time: None

Messiness Quotient: None

Materials: Your mail, magazines, a person besides yourself

Why to try it: This activity will give you time to read your own mail or a magazine while entertaining your baby and encouraging her to walk.

How to do it: While you sit in one chair reading your mail or sorting through it, give your baby pieces of mail you don't want and ask her to deliver it to another person in the room. When she does this, the other person in the room must reward her with a heartfelt thank you and another piece of mail to return to the first person. When you run out of mail, pull out those ubiquitous magazine subscription cards and have her deliver these back and forth.

PLAY CARDS

They can't shuffle, but they sure can play 52 Pickup.

Suggested Ages: One year and up

Your Child's Special Skills and Interests: Interested in sorting, turning pages, hinges

Preparation Time: None

Messiness Quotient: Medium

Materials: One deck of cards

Commonsense Caution: Babies aren't cheaters at cards, but they can be eaters of cards. Watch closely as they play.

Why to try it: It's a simple, cheap, and easy-to-put-your-hands-on toy.

How to do it: A simple deck of cards can be a great toy for a baby showing interest in hinges, turning pages, and other paper-related activities. Simply give baby the deck of cards when you read your mail or sort your own paperwork, and let her play at your feet, sorting, collecting, and tossing the cards up and down. Note: You'll probably have to help with the pickup part, and you'll definitely want to keep an eye out for card eaters. And of course, you should consider this deck of cards lost to the game closet and buy another set for yourself.

EXPERIMENT WITH GRAVITY

Quiet ways to see that what goes up does come down.

Suggested Ages: 18 months and up

Your Child's Special Skills and Interests: Able to throw things up in the air

Preparation Time: 5 minutes

Messiness Quotient: High

Materials: Bag of hypoallergenic feathers from the craft store, bag of cotton balls, individual paper tissues

Why to try it: This relatively quiet activity is perfect to try when you are on the phone: It keeps your child occupied, and the materials are naturally soundless.

How to do it: Grab a bag of feathers or a few tissues with one hand (holding the receiver in the other if you are talking on the phone) and show your child how to throw them up and

then watch them come down. It's a tiny thrill for you, but significant enough for him that he'll want to quickly collect all the fallen feathers or tissues and have you throw them (preferably on his head) again. Soon he'll be tossing them over himself all on his own, leaving you to wrap up your conversation.

LEAVE A NOTE

The Post-It note as a toddler toy.

Suggested Ages: 18 months and up

Your Child's Special Skills and Interests: Walking

Preparation Time: 10 minutes

Messiness Quotient: Medium

The Sibling Factor: Turn picking the notes up or putting them
out into a contest.

Materials: Pad of Post-It notes, washable markers or crayons

Why to try it: This is a great low-supervision activity for your
child while you catch up on desk work, and it can help your
child learn to follow directions or reinforce letter, color, or
shape recognition.

How to do it: In the most basic version of this activity, you
simply hand your child single Post-It notes and let her stick
them where she chooses. Once she's figured this part out, and
if she is old enough to follow simple directions, ask her to take
a note and put it in a specific place (on the refrigerator, the
doorknob, etc.). When she's stuck them all around the house,

she can fetch each one back as you request it. Or distribute the notes yourself, and ask your child to fetch a certain color or a note with a particular shape drawn on it. She can also draw her own notes on the papers, and then stick them around as decorations. Older toddlers and near-preschool age children might even begin making patterns with different-colored notes, alternating colors in a row on the wall. You will, of course, lose a pad of notes to these activities. But you'll probably gain 15 minutes of relatively uninterrupted time in return.

Travel Variation: Desperate to amuse your bored and cranky baby in the back seat? Let him "decorate" his surroundings with as many stick-on notes as he needs. They are easy to take down again. Or rip notes in two and wrap one end to the other and slip it over your fingers: Instant travel finger puppets!

TRY THREE EASY CRAFTS

Three simple-to-do and easy-to-clean-up art projects.

Suggested Ages: Two years and up

Your Child's Special Skills and Interests: Able to scribble and hold brushes and glue

Preparation Time: 10 minutes

Messiness Quotient: Medium

Materials: Construction paper, watercolor brush, washable markers, glue stick, scissors, tube of refrigerated biscuit dough

Why to try it: Your child is clamoring to paint or play with dough. You are too busy to orchestrate these messy activities. You can try these at the kitchen table with minimal supervision from afar.

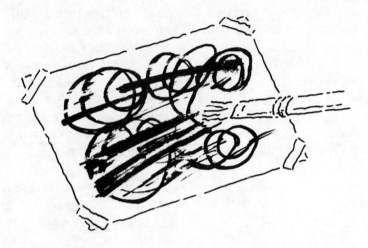

How to do it:

Water "Colors": Let your child scribble or draw with washable markers on a piece of construction paper. When he's completed his drawings (or is bored with the activity), hand him a cup of water and a paintbrush and let him brush over his drawings with the wet brush, blurring the lines and thereby—essentially—painting.

Glue on the Go: Quickly cut several pieces of construction paper into a half-dozen shapes and colors your child is learning: squares, circles, triangles, hearts, rectangles, and so forth. Then hand her a washable glue stick and let her glue and stick the shapes on another piece of paper.

Different Dough: For a quick modeling experience (with no messy crumbs under the table), break open a tube of biscuit, pie, or other commercially made refrigerator

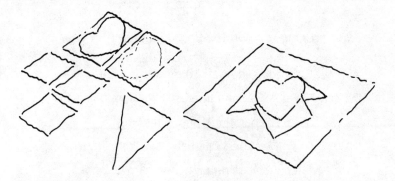

dough and donate it to the cause, tossing it out with a few cookie cutters and a lightweight rolling pin. Your kids will enjoy rolling, smashing, and molding it, and, if you choose, turning it into an edible treat. Just sprinkle on cinnamon and sugar and bake, serving the treats only to the artists whose little hands made them, of course.

WALK THE LINE

Put masking tape on the floor to design play courses.

Suggested Ages: 18 months and up

Your Child's Skills and Interests: Walking, balancing

Preparation Time: 5 minutes

Messiness Quotient: Medium

Materials: Masking tape, non-carpeted floor

Commonsense Caution: Test the tape you are using first to make sure it comes up off the floor. If you have access to drafting tape, this usually comes up well.

Why to try it: If you feel housebound, think about how your kids feel. By late afternoon, they are often ready for a change of scene. This simple activity can be just what they need to get through dinner with minimal supervision.

How to do it:

Grand Central Station: Build a superhighway across your kitchen floor. Lay tape in parallel lines across and around the floor. Kids will naturally want to follow the tape with their tiny cars. If you have any cardboard tubes, put them on the "highway" too, to serve as tunnels (tape them down). This same highway can also serve as a train track.

The Low Beam: Even very young children will walk across a board if it is laid on the ground in front of them. Unfortunately, adults will trip over this same board. To develop a safer "walking the line" project, lay two long strips of tape an inch or two apart on the floor. Encourage your kids to walk in between the strips once, and they'll likely do it again and again.

Kitchen Hideout: It doesn't take too much to make a hideout for toddlers. Simply mark a square with masking tape in a corner of your kitchen, with an opening for the "door." If you confined your kids to this space they'd hate it, but they'll love squishing inside with their toys by themselves and keeping you out.

PLAY BALL

When you are too busy to play, a bouncy, rolling ball is a great stand-in.

Suggested Ages: One year and up

Your Child's Special Skills and Interests: Walking, throwing

Preparation Time: None

Messiness Quotient: None

Materials: Balls, broom, empty trash can or laundry basket, string

> **Commonsense Caution:** Hard or heavy balls can hurt baby or damage your belongings and should be kept away from baby. You should also keep balls out of your home that are small enough to pose a choking hazard.

Why to try it: Babies love balls. Show them a few ways to play with them they may not have thought of, and they'll keep themselves busy for minutes on end.

How to do it: Keep a basket of balls of various sizes, textures, and materials easily accessible to babies one year old and up so they can invent their own games. Your ball collection should include a large (36 inches or so) but lightweight bouncy ball for baby to feel thrilled to be able to push or lift, as well as the following: soft felt balls, sponge balls, balls with nubs or long arm-like protrusions, blow-up balls, stuffed balls, and balls that squeak or ring or even talk and light up. You'll want to stay away from hard or heavy balls or the tiny rubber "super balls" that are wonderful fun to bounce but also pose a choking hazard for young children and can zoom back at baby with incredible force. Need a ball in a hurry? Crumple up a piece of paper into a ball and tape it closed with masking tape.

Broom Ball: Show your baby how to push a large bouncing ball around the room with a push or whisk broom.

Laundry Basket Ball: Show your toddler how to toss large or baseball-size balls into the wide and low target of a laundry basket or trash can.

Baby Tennis: Tack a tennis ball onto a 6-inch length of string, securing the other end around the arm of a chair or table high enough that the ball will still hang above your child's head. Now let your toddler hit away at the ball with a cardboard paddle constructed of two pieces of corrugated cardboard glued together for strength. Be sure to take the string-ball down when you have finished playing or can't supervise baby closely.

ROLL AROUND

When a paint roller is an iron, a race car—and more.

Suggested Ages: One year and up

Your Child's Special Skills and Interests: Walking

Messiness Quotient: None

Preparation Time: None

Materials: New paint roller

Why to try it: Watch baby creativity in action while you spin the salad for dinner as baby explores uses for a paint roller you may not have considered.

How to do it: Give baby a paint roller and let the fun begin. Watch as she rolls it around the floor, or on the wall, or tickles her legs or yours by rolling it across them. She can pretend-iron with a paint roller, or pretend-paint, of course. It also makes a great "engine" for rolling cars or balls across a floor.

MAKE A FORT

A room of their own—even in the kitchen—can make all the difference.

Suggested Ages: One year and up

Your Child's Special Skills and Interests:
Walking and crawling

Preparation Time: 15 minutes

Messiness Quotient: Medium to high

Materials: Large cardboard boxes, wooden dowels or broom/ mop handles, towels, blankets, pillows, string, scissors or sharp craft knife (for adult use only)

Why to try it: Your child will probably happily play alone in his new fort for at least a few minutes, and if you give him old toys in his fort, he'll see them in a new light in their new surroundings.

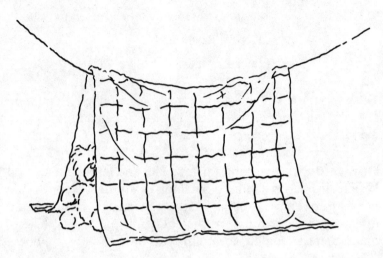

How to do it:

The Towel Tunnel-Tent: Suspend two pieces of string parallel to each other between two doorknobs and about 3 feet up. Drape towels over the top to provide a cozy tent inside. Take this tent down when you cannot closely supervise its use: Strings are a strangulation hazard.

The Indoor Tipi: Brace dowels or broom (or mop) handles against each other or against the wall, and cover them with a towel or sheet.

Boxed Houses: Save large boxes and cut windows and doors in them, connecting them with tape to make multi-room forts. If you'd like a collapsible, re-usable cardboard fort, cut out panels of cardboard and punch matching holes on all sides. When you want to build a fort, simply connect the panels using pipe cleaners, twist ties, or even screws and wing nuts. Velcro tabs also work well to connect the cardboard sheets and secure the hinges of doors and windows.

Permanent Forts: Storage closets look like small room-forts to kids. If you have the space, remove what is stored in a closet close to the kitchen, and turn it into a small playroom fort—and handy toy closet.

POP SOME BUBBLES

Two ways to pop bubbles and get exercise.

Suggested Ages: 18 months and up

Your Child's Special Skills and Interests: Walking

Preparation Time: 5 minutes

Messiness Quotient: Medium

Materials: Bubble solution with two bubble wands, bubble packing material

Commonsense Caution: Bubble solution can be slippery. Make sure your child has shoes on when he runs for bubbles.

Why to try it: This is a great way for your kids to get exercise with minimal exertion from you.

How to do it: Find any bubble wrap in the boxes you open at the end of the day? Put it on uncarpeted floor space and show your toddler that dancing and stomping make the bubbles pop. He could also try popping the bubbles with a wooden hammer from his hammering-board set. While you cook or read, you can also blow bubbles to your child, who, armed with a wand of his own, can run and dance and try to catch them.

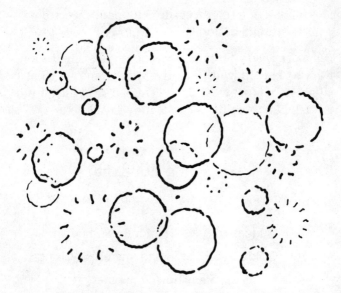

Homemade Bubble-Making Variation: To make your own, long-lasting, super-big bubble solution, you'll need two-thirds cup Dawn liquid dish soap, 1 tablespoon of glycerin (available at pharmacies), and a gallon of water. Let the solution sit overnight, and stir lightly before using.

GET INTO A STICKY SITUATION

Exploring the wonder and joy of sticky tape.

Suggested Ages: 18 months and up

Your Child's Special Skills and Interests: Able to manipulate
small objects with some precision

Preparation Time: 5 minutes

Messiness Quotient: Low

The Sibling Factor: If you have the time, your near-three-year-old or older will love making a sticky-tape letter using objects that begin with that letter. For instance, you could lay out cotton balls, caps, and clips to stick on a letter "C."

Materials: Double-sided tape, construction paper, and a variety of stickable objects (cotton balls, scraps of paper or candy wrappers, toothpicks, etc.)

Why to try it: This craft takes minutes for you to set up but can amuse baby for much longer.

How to do it: Place double-sided tape in strips on a piece of paper. If you'd like, you can have your strips form a letter or shape—or just slap them on. Now show your baby how he can pick up items and stick them onto the tape. He'll have made an amazing collage before he even realizes it.

JAZZ UP YOUR CHILD'S BLOCK PLAY

Keeping your child's blocks fresh and fun.

Suggested Ages: Two years and up

Your Child's Special Skills and Interests: Building block towers with ease

Preparation Time: 15 minutes

Messiness Quotient: Medium

Materials: 4-foot by 4-foot sheet of masonite from lumberyard, set of 75 to 100 blocks in varying lengths and shapes but uniform depth, toy cars, people, doll furniture, clean recyclables such as paper towel holders, oatmeal boxes, etc.

Why to try it: Block play helps children develop eye-hand coordination and fundamental math and spatial skills, and it inspires creativity, experimentation, and conversation. And blocks often keep children's attention even without a playmate or adult at their side.

How to do it: Because block play is so important, dedicate an out-of-the-way corner with a flat wood or vinyl surface to the purpose. If you don't have an uncarpeted area, pick up a piece of masonite at the lumberyard and use it for block play and storage: Just slide it—blocks and all—under a bed or couch. In addition to a set of blocks make a habit of furnishing a changing cast of props: Toy cars, people, doll furniture, or animals can inspire a toddler to turn their block structures into a house, barn, or parking garage. An empty paper-towel tube can become a tower (or, cut in half, a tunnel); an old oatmeal box, a silo; a margarine tub, a swimming pool.

MAKE A BRACELET

String beads on pipe cleaners.

Suggested Ages: Two years and up

Your Child's Special Skills and Interests: Able to string beads, not oral

Preparation Time: 5 minutes

Messiness Quotient: Low—unless the beads spill

Materials: Pipe cleaners, beads with a big enough hole to slip over them

Commonsense Caution: Not for use around children who put small objects in their mouth.

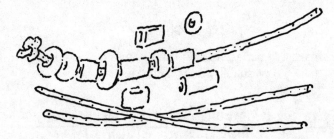

Why to try it: A great exercise in fine motor skills, this activity produces bracelets for your child and all of her stuffed animals. It is also much easier than stringing beads on thread, and will give your child a great feeling of success. For a great lightweight travel toy as well, put the beads and pipe cleaners in a plastic bag—and let your toddler gift the seatmates around her with a bracelet.

How to do it: Fold over the bottom of a pipe cleaner several times, until the lump is big enough that a bead will not slip over it. Now hand your child a cup of beads (don't give her more than a dozen at a time, so a spill will be easier to pick up) and show her how to put the beads on the pipe cleaner. She'll usually be able to string her beads along happily for several minutes. When she nears the end of the pipe cleaner, twist the two ends together for a bracelet for your child or a necklace for a stuffed bear.

TRY A 3-D PAINTING

Take your toddler's painting to a new dimension.

Suggested Ages: Two years and up
Your Child's Special Skills and Interests: Comfortable with painting

Preparation Time: 5 minutes

Messiness Quotient: High

Materials: Old boxes, mailing tubes, Styrofoam packing forms, washable paints, and paintbrushes

Why to try it: Painting objects—rather than flat pieces of paper—offers an intriguing new challenge for young artists who might otherwise turn up their nose at your suggestion that they paint a picture while you cook nearby.

How to do it: Keep a laundry basket or box in an out-of-the-way location where you can keep objects that can be repainted. Paints generally adhere well to Styrofoam packing shapes and can also be used on unprinted cardboard, such as brown paper cardboard boxes, bags, and tubes. To paint other materials—such as round oatmeal boxes or plastic or glass jars—cover them with taped-on construction paper.

BUILD A HOUSE OF STRAWS

Stick straws and clay together and play.

Suggested Ages: Two years and up

Your Child's Special Skills and Interests:
Sticking things together

Preparation Time: 5 minutes

Messiness Quotient: Medium

Materials: Home made or purchased play dough, drinking straws, scissors

Why to try it: This activity exercises fine motor skills and creativity, and requires little instruction once you show baby how it's done.

How to do it: Quickly roll play dough into a dozen large marble-size balls and cut all the drinking straws in half. (Note: You can show your child how to make the balls too, but this is often too difficult for young kids and has them frustrated before they even start.) Now show your child how she can connect the balls together using the straws, or simply make wild and unnamed free-form sculptures.

GIVE BABY THE RUN-AROUND

Let your child run for his supper.

Suggested Ages: Two years and up

Your Child's Special Skills and Interests: Running!

Preparation Time: 3 minutes

Messiness Quotient: Low

Materials: Large metal pan, bag of change

Commonsense Caution: Be sure your little run-
ner's route is clear of obstacles that might make
him trip, fall down, or break something as he runs.
And don't let children who are at all oral play with
coins, which are tempting (for some reason) for
them to put in their mouths and pose a choking
hazard. You can substitute, for example, small
balls or wooden blocks.

Why to try it: This activity lets your little bundle of energy
run his energy all off and allows him to practice counting—
and begin to understand the concept of numbers—at the same
time.

How to do it: Give your child's desire to run some purpose.
Establish a "race course" within view of where you are working, then have baby run back and forth (or round and round)
and drop a coin in the pan with a delightful clink each time
he passes the starting line. When he tires of this (and he may
keep going for a surprisingly long time) count up the pennies
to determine how many laps he ran.

PLAY WITH STICKY BLOCKS

Exciting construction with stick-on Velcro tabs.

Suggested Ages: Two years and up

Your Child's Special Skills and Interests: Stacking, sticking things
together

Preparation Time: 10 minutes

Messiness Quotient: Low

Materials: A set of lightweight wooden blocks, or lightweight, sturdy cardboard boxes, stick-on Velcro tabs, colored marker (optional)

Commonsense Caution: Small children who are still inclined to eat things can easily pull off these stick-on tabs and ingest them. Watch them closely or save this game for later.

Why to try it: The challenge of matching and sticking Velcro tabs together is usually absorbing for toddlers, keeping them happily pressing boxes or blocks together in search of the right combination for minutes on end. And of course, ripping the tabs apart has its own satisfaction for many toddlers, who will stick them together and pull them apart just to hear the rip.

How to do it: Quickly stick some Velcro tabs on a set of cardboard or other recyclable boxes that can be used as building-blocks or add them to a few real wooden blocks (after playtime you'll want to take the tabs off or keep these blocks separate from the rest, since the tabs make them uneven for stacking purposes). Now show your child how he can make things stick together by pressing the tabbed blocks together. If he is easily frustrated, color all the rougher-sided Velcro tabs with a marker and leave all the softer connecting tabs blank. This will help him more easily match the tabs that will stick together.

MAKE A SCULPTURE

Turn a special type of packing peanut into a wild sculpture.

Suggested Ages: Two and a half years and up

Your Child's Special Skills and Interests:
Sticking things together

Preparation Time: 5 minutes

Messiness Quotient: Medium

Materials: A damp sponge and cornstarch-peanut packaging—
the shapes look like packing peanuts but are tubular and get
sticky instantly when wet

> **Commonsense Caution:** These peanuts are technically edible (and FDA approved) but they could lodge in a small throat, so keep them away from children who might be tempted to eat them rather than stick them.

Why to try it: Before you quickly toss out every packing peanut you get in the mail, check to see if you've ended up with biodegradable packing peanuts. If so, you'll have an easy, unique craft that your child can try with very little help. It is also "totally cool."

How to do it: Show your child how to lightly touch the end of a cornstarch peanut to the damp sponge, making it instantly sticky (you can tell if you have cornstarch peanuts, because an accompanying note will indicate that they are biodegradable and will "melt" when wet). Do this to another peanut and stick the two sticky spots together. Soon your child will be making wild sculptures with the peanuts. (But be warned, if your baby gets them too wet they will melt into nothing.) When your child is done, drop them into a bowl of water and presto: They'll virtually disappear. For some kids, this is the "coolest" part.

HAVE A QUIET CONTEST

A little competition is good for the ears.

Suggested Ages: Two and a half to three years

Your Child's Special Skills and Interests: Whispering,

following rules

Preparation Time: None

Messiness Quotient: None

Materials: None

Why to try it: For the quiet, of course.

How to do it: Telling your child that you are both having a quiet contest often works much better than simply telling your child to be quiet. It turns what you want into a game rather than just another parent request, and the real quiet this activity affords is a break from the ordinary for everyone, including your child. It is key that you play along as well: Pretend to "forget" and almost talk before you catch yourself, tip-toe around the kitchen, and carefully and soundlessly set each dish in the sink. If you'd like, you can set the kitchen timer for a certain length of quiet and then see if you and your child can reach your goal together.

High-Tech Variation: Turn a tape recorder on during your contest and listen later to see who made the most noise.

Chapter Five

~~~~~~

BATH TIMES AND BEDTIMES

Slow and Simple Ways to Settle Down for Sleep

And now it is time for that great, marvelous calm to fall over your home. You hope. By the end of a long day, it is only natural to feel as if you are in a race against the clock, anxious to get your child tucked away in bed early enough so that you can have a few precious hours on your own or with your spouse.

This rushed feeling is only intensified by the fact that your child seems to be working against you during these busy hours, doing everything possible to delay the process of bed you are so diligently trying to hurry along. And the reality is, your child probably *is* working against you. Once your baby gets old enough to be able to fight sleep and stay awake (usually sometime around one year of age or even younger), he probably will. While you can think of nothing more wonderful than to snuggle down between the covers, your average toddler can think of nothing worse. Sleep means no more fun, no more being next to Mom and Dad. Sleep, then, is to be avoided at all costs.

Your child's desire to be with you (and to avoid sleep) may be even more difficult for you to fight if you've been away from him during the day. If you have, you may feel the need to use this limited time to reconnect in meaningful ways with him, and end up extending his bedtime in order to do this. Don't give in to these feelings: A regular bedtime and plenty of sleep are important to your child's health and development and general attitude (not to mention your own).

What you need is an evening game plan that is fun and family-oriented and lets everyone feel close but that doesn't stir up anyone's adrenaline so much that sleep is put off even further. Quiet and calming activities that lead your child unwittingly into relaxation and sleep and that make you feel you have had substantial interactions with him are the order of the night. Of course, clever, sleep-fighting creatures that most toddlers are, they may force you to change this game plan regularly.

Once your child catches on that this or that step means bed, he may start fighting sleep indirectly, by refusing to do the first or second step, like putting on pajamas or making sure that each step in the nightly ritual lasts longer and longer. At times like these, firmness and a no-negotiation posture—as well as allowing ample time for your child to calm down and mellow out—are essential.

In your mind, allocate a good 15 or 20 minutes (or however long it typically takes) for each bedtime step, then keep your eye on your watch and try your hardest to meet those targets. If you do, you'll avoid the dramatic and confusing change for your child that occurs when—after a leisurely dinner and bath—*bam!* with a look at the clock, you suddenly begin hurrying to cram all the bedtime activities into 5 minutes. When you rush your child, and she feels hurried, you are working against the tone you are trying to set of quiet relaxation and interrupting whatever close interactions you are having.

Of course, sometimes you actually are in a hurry. At times

like these—or when your child is being particularly reluctant—you may need to use out-and-out bribery. Offering your child something new and exciting to add to the bath and bedtime ritual is one way to lure him peacefully (and expediently) into the good night. On just such evenings try some of the activities described below. They provide mostly quiet, sharing times, and many have a high entertainment value. And they might be just what you need to get your child, or your children, to hop into the bath and, not much later, to slip under the covers. In fact, the sibling enjoyment factor of most of these activities is high—kids of all ages like stories and singing and playing in water—so if you can get older children to participate, everyone should be getting sleepy or at least calm at the same time.

The activities that follow also share other qualities tired picker-upper parents appreciate late in the day: None of them requires much preparation, and all have a messiness quotient of zero. When your child finally does go to bed and leaves the house to you alone, the last thing you need is more things to clean up.

WHAT TO DO DURING TONIGHT'S BATH

Commonsense Caution for All Bath-Time Activities: The bath is a wonderful but treacherous place for young children. Never leave your child unattended during a bath for even a moment. Drownings—usually in small amounts of water, such as the bath—are a leading cause of accidental death in children under three. The bath also makes for slippery feet and bodies, and with so many hard and unforgiving surfaces nearby, falls can be particularly hazardous. Finally, bath water can scald. When you have a young child in the house, turn the setting on your water heater down to 120 degrees or lower.

MEET YOUR KNEES

Suggested Ages: Three months and up

Your Child's Special Skills and Interests: Enjoying the bath

Preparation Time: None

The Sibling Factor: An older child can show off his greater knowledge, if he chooses to help you bathe baby.

Materials: None

Why to try it: Stripped of clothing, your baby will begin to discover his body during his baths. Why not be his tour guide?

How to do it: During your child's bath, take time to introduce him to various body parts while you wash him. Be silly. Lightly touch one knee to another to have them meet, saying "Right knee, meet left knee, how do you do?" Or show baby how his wrist lets his hand go up and down. Make up rhymes as you touch nose and then toes, lips, and hips. You'll be having fun, and baby will be hearing you talk while learning about what to call his various body parts, as well as about what they can do.

PLAY WITH YOUR TOYS

Suggested Ages: Nine months and up

Your Child's Special Skills and Interests: Sitting up in bath more or less on own

Preparation Time: 15 minutes

The Sibling Factor: Engage an older sibling in looking for unique and silly bath toys to add to the water tonight. You'll be surprised at what they come up with: Make sure they know you need to okay them before they go in the water.

Materials: Sponges, washcloths, funnels, used plastic containers of varying sizes (some with holes punched in bottom), floatable plastic dolls, plastic balls and figures, spray bottles, plastic measuring cups, small colander or sieve or slotted spoon, zip-sealing plastic bags, Latex or rubber gloves

Why to try it: Water play is fun; toys make it even more delightful.

How to do it: Before you give your baby a bath, open a kitchen or bathroom drawer or cabinet. Chances are, you'll find a new bath toy. After all, as long as it meets criteria of a safe plaything—no sharp edges, nothing to strangle baby, and too big to be a choking hazard—and the guidelines for water play (it won't be ruined when wet or mess up the bath water), almost any object takes on new interest when it is added to the bath. Nevertheless, some extemporaneous bath toys are decidedly more fun than others. The following are particularly good choices:

Washcloths: Soak them in water, and then use them for Peek-a-boo with the toys in the bath and for silly puppet making when draped over your hand.

Sponges: A pack of unused kitchen sponges, cut into shapes, make marvelous toys for baby. When wet, they can be stuck to the side of the tub or can be used by baby to wipe the tub while she's in it. Baby can also practice "filling them up" and then "wringing them out." Show her how a sponge can soak up water in one cup and then fill up another.

Sieves, the tops of sippy cups, and plastic containers of varying sizes with varying numbers of holes punched in the bottoms (use a hammer and nail): These all make wonderful bath water fountains. Show baby how to hold one sippy-cup top upside down while you pour water into it from above—then watch as the water drips out of the tiny holes. Or hold one plastic container with one hole over another plastic container with several holes in the bottom to make a succession of fountains.

Plastic bags: Fill a zip-closing plastic sandwich bag halfway full with water and seal it closed. Now give it to baby to hold, squish, and float, and to try to figure out how to open it. You can also put a small toy inside that baby can try to move back and forth; later, teach your child how to dump the water out of the bag and then refill it. You can also put a drop of food coloring in the bag with the water to add extra interest—it is perfectly harmless to dump in the bath with your baby. *Note: Since plastic bags can be a choking and suffocation hazard, always put them out of reach when bath play is done.*

Spray bottles: Children under two will probably have a hard time operating a spray bottle themselves (which can be a good thing for wannabe dry parents) but will still enjoy the casual squirt or puff of mist. A spray bottle can also serve to rinse soapy hair without getting it in baby's eyes.

Plastic Toys: Dry-land pretend toys can be particularly fun in the bath, where plastic horses, for instance, can do more than run: they can swim—and baby's baby gets a bath right along beside her.

Rubber or Latex Glove: Fill up a glove to make a water hand; poke a hole in a fingertip to make it squirt.

PAINT YOUR BELLIES

Suggested Ages: 9 months (you do the painting) and 18 months (they do the painting)

Your Child's Special Skills and Interests: Learning about color, possibly painting

Preparation Time: 10 minutes

The Sibling Factor: Kids of all ages like to paint themselves; they'll love helping paint baby too.

Materials: Food coloring, hypoallergenic liquid baby soap or lotion

Commonsense Caution: Be sure painting occurs below the neck only: Keep stinging soap away from tender eyes.

Why to try it: A baby's belly offers a wide and wonderful canvas.

How to do it: Pour a tablespoon of your child's regular liquid body soap or shampoo into several small paper cups. Now add a drop or two of food coloring to each cup and stir. If your child is under a year old, put him in the bath and start finger-painting him yourself, telling him about the colors and shapes you are drawing on his belly. If your baby is a toddler, strip your child down, cover the bathroom floor with towels, and have the bath ready to go. Now pull out the "paints" and let your child dig in with his fingers, smearing and drawing the paint all over himself—and getting one good look at his creation in the mirror—before being dropped in the tub to wash it all off.

Rubber Duck Variation: You can also give your child a selection of soapy paints and let him paint, with a brush, his favorite bath toys while he is the bathtub. First, he paints the yellow duck blue, for instance, then he gets to wash it all off.

WASH YOUR HANDS

Suggested Ages: One year and up

Your Child's Special Skills and Interests: Finger play and rhymes, sitting up well in bath

Preparation Time: None

Materials: Washable markers, washcloths

Why to try it: It's always more fun to wash when you can actually see yourself get cleaner.

How to do it: Tonight, give your child permission to write on herself with washable markers, and mark on your own fingers at the same time if you wish—it will come off while you bathe your child, after all. Mark each fingertip with a blotch of color (for a one-year-old), or write a letter or number or silly face on each digit of an older child. Now re-word some of your favorite finger plays and play them in the bath. Instead of "Where is tall man?" sing "Where Is Yellow Man?" or "Where

Is Number One?" Or sing the "Itsy-bitsy spider" song and watch the colored fingers climb up the water spout—before dousing them from above with a cupful of rain. You can also make up finger plays yourself, with simple dialogue that instructs this finger or that one to scrub baby's nose or touch baby's belly button. This exercise also gives you and baby an easy-to-read signal about when bath time is over: when your fingers are all clean.

HAVE A DOUBLE-BUBBLE BATH

Suggested Ages: One year and up

Your Child's Special Skills and Interests: Enjoying bath, sitting on his own most of the time

Preparation Time: None

The Sibling Factor: Let an older sibling blow the bubbles for the younger child to catch, while you get a little clandestine cleaning accomplished.

Materials: Bubble bath and bubble wands

Commonsense Caution: Make certain the bubble bath you use is hypoallergenic and made for babies' sensitive skin. Keep all bubbles out of little eyes—the soap stings, regardless of what the labels say.

Why to try it: Babies love bubbles, and the bath is a perfect place for them to indulge this affection.

How to do it: After you pour bubbles into the bath, pour a little of the pure solution into a cup and dip and blow with a bubble wand. And if you don't have a bubble wand handy, you can quickly fashion one out of a pipe cleaner—it will work just as well.

PAINT YOUR NAILS

Suggested Ages: 18 months and up

Your Child's Special Skills and Interests: Painting

Preparation Time: None

The Sibling Factor: Older siblings are only too happy to do the painting; they may not appreciate a younger child's sloppier paint job on themselves, however.

Materials: Washable watercolor paints and tiny brushes, or commercial "peel-off" nail polish available at toy stores

> **Commonsense Caution:** Don't use real nail polish on young children. The remover is harsh on baby skin, and the actual product absolutely doesn't wash out.

Why to try it: Using washable "nail polishes" turns this popular activity into a thoroughly manageable event for both mess-conscious parents and their little kids, who love to see the paint on their nails—even if it is also all over their fingertips, too. Plus, this relaxing activity requires sitting still whether you are the painter or the painted, which helps slow things down before bed.

How to do it: Put down a towel to protect the area around where you'll be working. Remove most of your child's clothing (the bath is coming soon), and start painting his or her nails with either regular washable paint (applied with a small brush) or washable, peel-off nail polish, available at many toy stores. If you haven't painted baby's nails before, you might start by painting her toes, which are easier to keep still than wriggling fingers. Then paint her fingernails. When you have finished, let her try to paint your nails. If she still wants to paint more, strike a bargain: Tell her to get in the bath and wash it all off, and you'll re-paint her nails when she's in her pajamas. For many enthusiastic manicurists and manicure receivers, this is all the incentive they'll need to jump in and out of the bath and be on their way to bed in no time.

JUST PLUMB FUN

Suggested Ages: 18 months and up

Your Child's Special Skills and Interests: Balls and splashes

Preparation Time: 15 minutes

Materials: One foot of two-inch diameter PVC pipe, two two-inch diameter P-trap pipe fittings (both available at hardware stores), less than two inch diameter ball, duct tape

Why to try it: From the disappearing ball to the splash at the end, this activity offers plenty of bath time thrills.

How to do it: Tape the two fittings to the end of the pipe. Once your child is in the bath, hold the pipe on the edge of the tub, and let her put the ball inside. It will disappear for a moment (and rattle along, if it is a hard ball) and then appear with a splash back in the tub.

FLOAT YOUR BOATS

Suggested Ages: Two years and up

Your Child's Special Skills and Interests: Sitting on own securely in bath

Preparation Time: 20 minutes

The Sibling Factor: Boat making and races will remain passions well into the grade-school years; take care that an older sibling doesn't get too competitive or frustrated with a younger child's more easygoing attitude about the whole affair.

Materials: Margarine tubs and lids; plastic banana-split bowls; foam produce trays or boxes (such as those mushrooms are sold in); squares of Styrofoam; plastic straws; scissors; corks; flat, rounded-tip toothpicks; hole punch; tape; and glue.

Commonsense Caution: If boats come apart in the bath, be sure to remove debris (especially toothpicks, if you used them) from the bath so they won't poke an innocent bather.

Why to try it: What better incentive to hurry into the bathroom can you offer a toddler than a boat race?

How to do it: Even the simplest boats are exciting for toddlers. Tape a drinking-straw mast and paper flag to a margarine tub and you've got a craft that's perfectly satisfactory. A square of Styrofoam, similarly adorned, is even more buoyant. Or try something more complex: Working with your child, use rounded-tip, flat toothpicks to connect corks and create a seaworthy raft. Make several of these simple boats and discuss which one will work the best. Your toddler won't be able to wait to get in the tub and splash or blow at them all to see which will be the first to cross the finish line. Just be sure to lay down extra towels beside the race course—you can count on a whole lot of splashing going on.

DO MATH IN THE BATH

Suggested Ages: Two years and up

Your Child's Special Skills and Interests: Dipping and pouring

Preparation Time: 10 minutes

The Sibling Factor: Involve an older child in this activity by turning it into a pretend tea party (don't drink!) or factory water machine.

Materials: Plastic funnels and spoons, small plastic lids, many sorts and sizes of plastic containers with lids; empty, clean pill bottles; clean plastic juice jugs; old plastic scoops from laundry

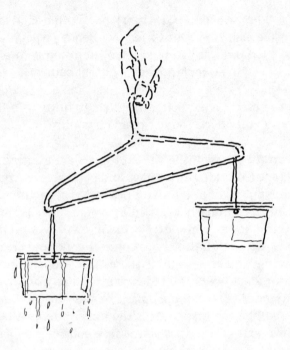

detergent boxes; empty plastic containers. Also: a plastic clothing hanger, string, and two equal-size plastic margarine or cottage cheese containers.

Why to try it: Pouring water back and forth between various sizes of containers is a key experience in beginning to understand measurement, an important early math skill.

How to do it: Clear out the other bath toys tonight and provide your young math scientist with a selection of containers. Show him how to pour from one to another, and let him experiment with moving water from a tall, thin container to a wide, short one. As tedious as this seems to adults, many small children particularly enjoy filling containers with small plastic spoons, or using a small lid to scoop water into and out of a bottle. Funnels are also useful for pouring water into small containers. All of this pouring and scooping will help your child understand volume; as your child nears three or more, you can add counting and estimating to the exercise. Have your child count or guess how many spoonfuls it will take to fill or empty a bowl.

Advanced Variation: In addition to experimenting with measurement and volume, you can construct a simple scale to begin to help teach your child balance. Punch holes in each side of two equal-size margarine or cottage cheese containers, then hang them with string from each end of a plastic hanger. While you hold the contraption over the bath water, let your child experiment with adding water to the cups on each side. At first, the scales will immediately tip—most likely, to your child's delight. But as she plays, she may become increasingly intrigued with trying to achieve some degree of balance.

ENJOY SOME SIPHON SILLINESS

Suggested Ages: Two years and up

Your Child's Special Skills and Interests: Squirting water, watching water fall

Preparation Time: 5 minutes

The Sibling Factor: Let an older sibling help you set up this contraption and add the food coloring drops.

Materials: Several feet of one-fourth-inch diameter plastic tubing (available at most hardware stores for about 20 cents a foot) and a bucket; food coloring (optional)

Commonsense Caution: Only use the siphon to move clean water into the bath. Don't suck up dirty bath water or let your child do so either.

Why to try it: Although even a wise old three-year-old won't be mature enough to appreciate the "cool" physics of siphoning (the water moves up and down—on its own!), he'll enjoy this activity, nonetheless.

How to do it: While you fill the bath, catch a clean bucket of warm water and set it aside. Once your child is in the bath, show him how you can move water from the outside tub into the inside one. Place your bucket slightly higher than the bottom of the bath. Start the water moving up the tube and out of the bucket by sucking gently on the end that will go into your child's bath (if possible, without your child seeing you and wanting to do the same). Once the water begins to flow, drop the tube into the tub. Now, for extra excitement, change the colors of the water as it enters the tub, by adding drops of food coloring to your outside tub. Watching the colors swirl and mix in the tube is quite exciting; you might just have to do the whole thing over again and again.

MAKE FACES, WEAR TOWELS

Suggested Ages: Two and a half years and up

Your Child's Special Skills and Interests: Dressing up, play acting, becoming inventive physically

Preparation Time: None

Materials: A large mirror big enough and low enough for two, towels of different sizes

Why to try it: This is a fun way to "wrap up" your family's evening bath time.

How to do it: After the bath, while you pat dry your child's hair and face, you can both sit in front of the mirror and make faces and play with towels. Drop a washrag on your heads as a "hat"; curl another towel around your shoulders as a "robe." Then, while you surreptitiously get the before-bed hygiene taken care of—hair combed and dried, lotion applied—keep looking in the mirror with your child and making faces for him to imitate. You can even keep him facing forward as long as you only make a face when you are looking in the mirror—he won't be able to take his eyes off of you.

WHAT TO DO BEFORE BED TONIGHT

START OFF WITH A MASSAGE

Suggested Ages: Birth and up

Your Child's Special Skills and Interests: None

Preparation Time: None

The Sibling Factor: An older child can be your assistant, warming the lotion in his hands before passing it to you.

Materials: Petroleum jelly or baby lotion, towel

Why to try it: Your touch offers your child vitally important stimulation that will affect all of her development. Making a massage part of your evening routine relaxes both baby and you before bed.

How to do it: Before you change baby into her pajamas but while she has a clean diaper on, lay her on a towel in a warm place and begin to gently rub baby-safe hypoallergenic lotion or oil (warm it in your hands before applying) on her arms, legs, chest, and back. Your touch should be firm but gentle. Make small circles with your hands as you touch baby's back and chest, run your hands up and down her legs and arms. Don't massage baby's belly: This kind of firm touch on the stomach can disturb digestion. Your child's reactions will quickly let you know which movements she enjoys and which might tickle a bit too much to be comfortable.

Advanced Variation: As your child reaches the age of two or three, she will enjoy giving you a massage. After you massage her, let her rub your arms and hands with lotion. Just be sure to control the amount of lotion your child puts on, or you'll have a whole lot of rubbing *off* to do.

SING A SONG

Suggested Ages: Birth and up

Your Child's Special Skills and Interests: None

Preparation Time: None

The Sibling Factor: It's likely your older child may know songs you can't remember. Let him help sing.

Materials: None

Why to try it: The most important thing you need to know about singing to your child is that your child is the most appreciative audience you'll ever have. Your voice may be two octaves off, your tune repetitive, your lyrics made up and non-rhyming. Your child won't care. This is love in its truest form. Enjoy it.

How to do it: Buy a collection of lullabies and listen to them yourself for a while in the car or the kitchen. Once you find a tune that sticks in your head, try to sing it enough times that you'll be able to remember it. Even knowing one lullaby is enough to start, although you'll want a few more than that eventually. Still, hearing one of these regular tunes can become a kind of calming signal to your child that sleep time is near once she becomes used to it. To make it more bearable for you to sing over and over again, change the lyrics as you go along. Insert your child's name or your dog's name, for example. Or change all the words. You'll find rhymes—sometimes not so good ones, but rhymes—as you go along. And the repetitiveness of the tune may just work to your advantage: As she listens to the tune, over and over, she'll have no choice but to drop into slumber.

LOOK AT PICTURES

Suggested Ages: Nine months and up

Your Child's Special Skills and Interests: Enjoying looking at photographs of people

Preparation Time: None

Materials: Family scrapbooks (the sturdier, the better)

Commonsense Caution: If you are particularly concerned about the condition of your photo-

graphs and have an eager-to-touch-everything
child, encase a few in a sturdy plastic-paged book
that will stand up to baby's loving touch.

Why to try it: Babies are drawn to photographs of people.
Why not show them photos of people you actually know?

How to do it: Bring a sturdy photo album with you to story
time tonight. (If such an item doesn't exist in your home, a
dozen or so individual photographs will work as well—though
baby may want to take them from your grasp—so don't bring
irreplaceable ones.) As you look at the photographs, storytelling will come naturally, making this a great activity for the just-
getting-started teller of tales.

TELL A STORY

Suggested Ages: One year and up

Your Child's Special Skills and Interests: Listening well

Preparation Time: 5 minutes

The Sibling Factor: Older siblings enjoy a good story too and can
provide the inspiration you need if your younger child can't talk
too well yet.

Materials: None

Why to try it: Listening to oral stories requires that your child
imagine what things look like as you talk, rather than relying
on a printed illustration. It's an important skill, and one that
you can reinforce nicely with an evening story. Storytelling
also allows you an opportunity to share information about
your own childhood; to reiterate (in story form) a point you've

been trying to make with your child; and to discover, through the stories he requests or responds to, what interests he has.

How to do it: The first thing you need to know about telling a story to the under-three set is this: You don't necessarily have to have a point to make. Oral stories for children under three can be simple slices of life, description-filled memories, or stories with continuing characters that you can develop over time. Just remember that any story you come up with will almost surely be delightful to your child, because while you tell the story, you are talking to him in his room one on one. What else could he ask for? If you need inspiration to get started, consider the following strategies.

Your childhood: Describe your childhood room, your special hiding places, your favorite hideouts. Be sure to lengthen the story with every small detail, no matter how insignificant. Chances are, the very fact that you remember certain details means they have special resonance for most children, including your own. And fixing their imagination on first one detail and then another is exhausting for their sleepy little minds, helping those eyelids to get droopier. As you tell the story, don't worry about a beginning or ending or even a plot. Simply hearing about your childhood is all the story your children will need.

Your animals: Often your current family pet—or an animal you had yourself in childhood—can become a wonderful character for a story. Simply put the animal in an unusual situation and the story will tell itself. Tell about the time Jasper the dog went skiing. (It was an accident, really, he stepped on two pieces of wood and started sliding—and didn't stop until he flew right over a hill and smack into a snowman.) And about the time

Sadie the cat was scared by a mouse. (Basically, the mouse said, "Boo.")

Your job: Explain to your child in simple and upbeat terms what you do for a living. Tell him what you like and dislike about it, what's fun and what's hard. By simplifying what you do and talking about it to your child in this way, you will demystify where you go during the day, and you might just discover a few things about your job yourself.

MAKE A BABY TAPE

Suggested Ages: One year and up

Your Child's Special Skills and Interests: Laughing, attempting speech

Preparation Time: 5 minutes

Materials: Cassette tape, tape player that records

Why to try it: Save the first sounds of your child's speech and, later, the real words and stories.

How to do it: Keep a tape player and blank cassette handy for bedtime. As you sit curled up, reading and talking, these are some of the best times to record your child's first words and attempts at conversation. When you play back a little of what is said, she may just be inspired to talk even more.

TRY SPECIAL ACTIVITIES FOR
SPECIAL BOOKS

Suggested Ages: One year and up

Your Child's Special Skills and Interests: Enjoying being read to, sitting quietly

Preparation Time: 15 minutes

The Sibling Factor: An older sibling can act as your assistant, pulling out materials while you read the book.

Materials: Variable, depending on book

Why to try it: Many young children are virtually serial readers: They want to read the same book, over and over, and in just the same way. To vary the experience for you—and add a little excitement for your child—read the same books if your child insists, but add an extra activity occasionally to make it special.

How to do it: If the following examples don't include one of your child's favorite titles, perhaps they'll still inspire you to come up with activities related to your child's special books.

Harold and the Purple Crayon, by Crockett Johnson. Have your own big purple crayon, of course, and let your child draw with it while you read. When you've finished reading, draw a simple picture of your child's bed, and then tuck one of him under the one-dimensional covers.

The Rainbow Fish, by Marcus Pfeister. Bring a small flashlight to bed, and shine the light on the glimmering, shimmering scales of Rainbow Fish as you turn the pages.

Good Night, Moon, by Margaret Wise Brown. Read this book in the kitchen, right before bed, with your own bowl full of bedtime mush.

The Shape of Me, by Dr. Seuss. After you read this book, cast your own shadow shapes on the wall by bringing along a flashlight and a bag full of objects. If your child is close to three, she might even be able to guess the identity of some of the shadow shapes.

Yertle the Turtle, by Dr. Seuss. You can graphically represent the topple of the turtles by building a block tower to represent the turtle stack as you read. At the end, pull out Mack, the bottom turtle, to show the dramatic results of Yertle's power issues.

Draw Me a Star, by Eric Carle. This wonderful book about the imagination of an artist offers great inspiration for any child. Draw along with the book yourself, or encourage your child to draw while you read.

The Three Little Kittens. Bring a pair of your child's mittens to bed with you to use as props while you read this classic rhyme. Put them on and take them off and hide them as the story dictates. Many Mother Goose stories and rhymes lend themselves to this kind of play-acting. Before reading about the old woman who lived in a shoe, stuff the largest adult boot in your home with tiny dolls. Even a young child will enjoy pulling them out as you read, while imagining herself living in a shoe.

ROCK-A-BYE, BABY

Suggested Ages: One year and up
Your Child's Special Skills and Interests: Able to hold on
Preparation Time: None

The Sibling Factor: You won't want to introduce this activity if
your older child is too heavy to do this with as well: He'll
definitely want to try.

Materials: One sturdy regular-size blanket, two able adults

Why to try it: This is a sweet and snuggly family-bonding
activity. And it's fun, too.

How to do it: Fold your blanket in half, and have your child
lay down on top. Now you and your partner grab the two corners of the blanket at your child's head and feet and lift (using
your knees, not your back), creating a hammock effect for your
child. Gently swing your child back and forth while you talk
or sing and look down at him. Don't ever let this become
roughhouse play, and don't do this outside of bedtime hours
(you want to save it as something special to look forward to
for sleep time). When you, your partner, or your child becomes
tired, use your swing to gently lift your child onto the bed or
into the crib before story time.

READ IN A NEW DIMENSION

Suggested Ages: 18 months and up

Your Child's Special Skills and Interests: For young readers who like to look—and touch

Preparation Time: 20 minutes

The Sibling Factor: An older child may enjoy texturizing baby's books as an afternoon craft project.

Materials: Scissors, glue or tape, and scraps of various textures and colors: foil, sandpaper, felt, fake fur, etc.

Why to try it: This is a great way to give a new touch to an old book.

How to do it: Over the course of a few days, collect scraps of materials of different colors and textures: a piece of sandpaper, a scrap of felt or silk, a piece of aluminum foil, a handful of cotton balls, a ribbon, and so forth. Now open up one of your child's favorite books. Look carefully at the images and imagine what they might feel like. Then place the appropriate scrap of material inside the pages, or glue it, cut to fit, directly onto the illustration. If you don't want to permanently alter the book, just paper-clip the scrap to the appropriate page and hand it to your child to feel as you read.

Special Book Lover's Variation: If your child loves certain books so much he insists on bringing them to his bed, but you worry about hard corners poking him or disrupting his sleep, turn a few of your hardbacks into softcovers. Simply pick up a square of fake fur at your fabric or craft store and glue it on. (You may even find self-adhesive squares at craft stores.) Your child's favorite story is now effectively a "stuffed book."

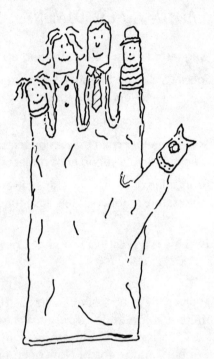

PUT ON A PUPPET SHOW

Suggested Ages: 18 months and up
Your Child's Special Skills and Interests: Enjoying stories
Preparation Time: 5 minutes
The Sibling Factor: Let an older child help you put on the show.
Materials: Hand or finger puppets

Why to try it: Puppet shows add an extra, dramatic dimension to the nighttime story hour.

How to do it: You can often find a "script" for your puppet show in the books you have already read to your child. If not, use the puppets to act out a scenario that you and your child experienced during the day. Have one puppet paint, make a mess, and cry—and then help to clean the mess up. Have another puppet eat everything for dinner and ask for more and more. Just as in storytelling, puppet shows for the very young don't have to be long on plot if they are full of silly voices, strange noises, and slapstick moves.

No-Puppet Variation: If you don't have a ready collection of puppets, make some. Draw faces on the fingertips of an inexpensive fabric glove with a permanent marker, and attach felt and yarn features with glue or tiny stitches. If you want to make puppets that fit anyone in the family, cut off the decorated fingers from the glove so they'll slip over digits of any size.

DRAW A PICTURE

Suggested Ages: 18 months and up

Your Child's Special Skills and Interests: Talking, telling stories

Preparation Time: None

The Sibling Factor: If baby isn't talking well yet, let the older sibling call the shots in this activity, and baby can enjoy watching.

Materials: Pad of paper, colored pencil or markers

Why to try it: For your child, watching his words become a picture (however crude) is nothing short of magic. And, like storytelling to young children, technical expertise is unnecessary. Even if you can only draw the crudest of figures, your child will almost certainly be entranced. Remember, your child has yet to master the stick figure himself.

How to do it: While you sit armed with a pad of paper and pencil, let your child call the shots. Let him tell you what he wants you to draw, detail by detail. Should the horse have a long tail or a short one? Should the man wear a hat or a feather? Being able to choose the direction of the drawing and see the results of his choices will almost certainly be inspirational, as well as very conversational. Ask your child what might be missing on a particular picture, and discuss why the horse should have a necklace on. The resulting before-bedtime talk and the silly picture will almost certainly amuse you both.

HELP YOUR BABY KEEP A DIARY

Suggested Ages: Two years and up

Your Child's Special Skills and Interests: Drawing, talking

Preparation Time: 5 minutes

The Sibling Factor: An older child can easily draw alongside a younger one.

Materials: Blank book, crayons, scissors, clear tape

Why to try it: This activity helps your child develop an early connection between the spoken and the written word. And the result is a wonderful keepsake for both of you.

How to do it: While you play during the day, set aside a few flat, glueable souvenirs: a page-size portion of a finger-painting or other art project, an instant photograph of what you've been up to, and so forth. You can glue these into a blank book and then "take dictation" as your child tells you about the item and what it means to her. Or simply let your child draw images of whatever comes to her in her book. When she has finished, you can write down what each sketch represents, if anything, underneath it. It's important that you don't try to guess what the drawings represent, or suggest anything—you'll probably be wrong. Simply admire the work, and if she wants to tell you something about it, write it down.

TURN ON A LIGHT IN THE DARK

Suggested Ages: Two years and up

Your Child's Special Skills and Interests: Becoming aware of light and darkness

Preparation Time: None

The Sibling Factor: All you'll need is an extra flashlight to keep everyone happy.

Materials: Small flashlights for you and your child

Why to try it: Around the age of two or three, the state of the lights in your house—and in his room, in particular—may become of utmost interest to your child. In addition to leaving on or turning off a particular light, giving your child control of one small flashlight can help.

How to do it: Before bed tonight, give your child a small flashlight (soft and small enough that he won't bonk himself on his head with it) to take along. The type that squeezes on and off is sometimes easiest for kids to operate, though some kids have difficulty finding the right place to squeeze. If this is the case, try a regular flashlight, and you can be the one to turn it on and off. Be sure to bring a flashlight for yourself as well. First, read the evening's books by flashlight. Then, before bed, quietly experiment with your flashlights. Shine the light through your hands or cheeks. Have your light chase your child's light in a game of ceiling tag. Let your child experiment with making the light bigger and smaller. Shine the light on things like the mirror or other reflective surfaces. Make a few simple hand shadows. Then send your child to bed to play alone with his flashlight for a few minutes. Once your child has fallen asleep, you can come back in and turn it off, and remove it from his bed or crib if you wish.

LOOK AHEAD TO TOMORROW

Suggested Ages: Two and a half years and up

Your Child's Special Skills and Interests: Becoming aware of time

Preparation Time: None

The Sibling Factor: An older child will enjoy seeing a list of his future activities as well.

Materials: Paper, pencil, see-through container with top (big enough for hands to reach inside)

Why to try it: At around this age, some children can be lured to bed by the prospect of what awaits them once they hurry up and get their sleep over with.

How to do it: As you cuddle in bed or the rocking chair, take a few moments to look ahead to what exciting things the next day might bring. You'll learn about what your child enjoys in this process, and he'll learn a bit about what your days involve. If you'd like, write down everything you and your child want or need to do on a list (include even small things, like "brush teeth," or "feed dolly her breakfast"). This makes your plans for the next day seem more certain and exciting to your child, and gives you a list to operate from the minute you get up.

Chapter Six

~~~~~~~

OUTINGS

Bringing Along Baby—and Fun

Wherever you go with baby, outings with a very young child are almost guaranteed to be both exhausting and exciting, fun and frustrating. But regardless of the ups and downs, a change of scene usually makes the effort all worthwhile. Outings expose your baby to new and different experiences and learning opportunities than you can provide at home and, perhaps even more important, get you out of the house as well.

When you plan outings, think of how you would plan a day running around with a friend. Be sure to provide a mix of activities to suit both you and your child. If you need to run errands, try to schedule a stop at the pet store. If you spend the morning at the playground with your child, reward yourself with a lunch outside at your favorite café. Sometimes even the smallest incentives are all your toddler will need to help her keep a positive attitude while you get through your errands.

And although a lollipop will sometimes quiet a dissatisfied child, there's no need to get in the habit of buying your child's compliance or happiness. Nor do your child-centered activities need to be big events like parades or festivals, which can be exhausting and overwhelming for everyone. Simple diversions from your route are often easier and just as interesting and can often keep your child's attitude upbeat longer. Shop at a grocery where your child can see live lobsters in a tank, for instance; change your route to pass by a construction site where a crane is operating; or stop by your local library for story hour. Several of these short, easy-to-navigate outings, breaking up your day out of the house, are often as exciting for your child as one big, exhausting one. And they are also more personal, and more about building your relationship with your child. Think about your own relationships and friendships: It's fun to go out to big, exciting events—but not all the time. Like your child, you want a balance between big events and small get-aways, between going out and just staying at home hanging out with the people you love.

When you do go out you'll have to have on hand adequate supplies (especially food, clothing, baby carriers, and toys that fit your outing) and be ready to do a fair amount of entertaining your child yourself. Because although a change of scene will sometimes completely occupy your baby's attention for the duration, outings are not necessarily a total break from having to amuse your baby. In fact, you may find yourself needing to interact and entertain him more than usual as you show him all the new things around him, and you may have to protect him from hazards that might not be present at home. Indeed, outings can often be much more exhausting than just staying home.

But in many ways, the extra demands involved are why outings with a young child are so much fun and so rewarding. Showing a young child the ocean for the first time, or the snow, the animals at the zoo, or even a swing set at the playground:

This is the kind of experience that makes parenthood seem so magical and worthwhile.

In fact, this magic can wear off on older siblings as well, who will often love to show a younger child the sights that they believe they know so well and to share the activities they did as "young" children. The following outing-based activities are appropriate for babies as well as many older children, but are especially exciting as ways to enhance your child's first-time experiences, making memories that you will clearly remember, even if your two-year-old may not.

WHAT TO DO WHEN YOU GO TO . . .

The Beach

While the beach is full of things that are naturally interesting to your child, because of the assorted dangers there—from drowning to stepping on a sharp shell to getting a really bad sunburn—your attention is going to have be on your child, regardless of her ability to amuse herself. This is a good thing: Having a child gives you license to do all of the fun things with sand and surf that you haven't been able to enjoy since you were at the beach with your parents.

And there's more good news. Like all worthwhile outings, the beach itself provides most of what you'll need in terms of toys. In addition to whatever you always bring to the beach, you need to tote along only a good source of shade, plenty of sun block for babies over six months (the spray-on kind is a godsend for parents of sunscreen resisters), all your regular baby food and equipment, plus plenty of fresh water to drink. You'll also want the following extras for sand play: plastic cookie cutters, spoons and knives, a hand-sized shovel, a wooden spoon, a plastic sieve, a bucket, and a few old yogurt and margarine containers. Messiness, naturally, isn't a factor— just try to leave as much sand as you can at the beach, and cover your car seats with towels to catch the rest.

Six Months and Up

Start off with a sunscreen smear. You'll need a towel and child-safe, waterproof sunscreen and at least two adults to one child. Have one adult lie down, and the other can pour a pool of sunscreen onto his or her stomach or back. Now let the child help you finger-paint the lotion-covered adult with sunscreen. Let the child make designs, and stay on hand so both of you can rub it in. When you have finished with the first adult, try the next one. Then, of course, it will be the child's turn. Always make this your first beach game, and consider doing it before you leave for the beach for ultimate effectiveness. You'll be setting a good example for your child, having fun, and getting sunscreen on the whole family.

Nine Months and Up

◐ Create treasures from the sea while you soak up the sun. Make your own rattle for a young child by stringing a seashell rattle. All you need are shells with holes in them and a pack of dental floss. While your baby amuses herself with the sand and sea, you can idly search for shells. Then string them together with dental floss and use them as a rattle bracelet for baby on the way home. Of course, watch young children closely—you don't want them swallowing the shells of their handmade rattle. As your child gets

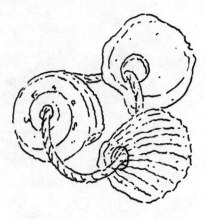

older, around three, she might be able to string her own shells, and older siblings might make whole jewelry ensembles. To make stringing easier at any age, tie one end of the floss to a tiny stick (a toothpick will work) to serve as a needle.

◐ Make sand cookies at the beach. All you need is a set of plastic cookie cutters and presses. These can provide hours of amusement at the beach for toddlers as they decorate sand sculptures, bake sand cookies, or simply press imprints in the sand at water's edge, then watch as the waves quickly wash them away.

◐ Mix up a batch of sand soup. All you need is a bucket, a sieve, and an eager pourer and digger of sand. Water and sand are truly magical combinations as far as the younger set is concerned. Pour a bucket of water into the sand. Where did it go? Let them try to mix up a sand soup by slowly adding sand to a bucket of water. Then make dribble

decorations by pulling up handfuls of the saturated sand.
A sieve can help them see the difference between wet and
dry sand as they watch what sand goes through the sieve
and what sand doesn't.

One Year and Up

○ Toddle and twist. Let your one-year-old, who's walking
steadily, try out his new skills by following in your foot-
steps. Remember the game twister? Try a version of it with
your toddler. Can they put their feet in your footprints?
Their hands in your handprints? This activity is a wonderful combination of great fun and great exercise for you
both.

◐ Go ahead and walk the plank. Kids have an early instinct for walking along lines. Using a long stick, draw out lines and then shapes and see if your toddler can walk along your winding course.

◐ Carry a big stick. Make a habit of finding a sturdy, straight, blunt-ended stick immediately upon your arrival at the beach. A stick of 2 to 3 feet in length is often the best beach toy children can have. They can use it to draw designs in the sand, let it drag behind them as they walk to make a trail, or dig out trenches. Before you begin to play, tell your child that the stick goes away if he doesn't follow one important rule: *No running with the stick in his hand. Falling on a straight stick can be dangerous, even if the end is blunt.*

Two Years and Up

◐ Run for shade. Help your child burn off extra energy while learning the difference between sun and shade, by holding a Race for the Shade as you walk or run along the beach. This will only work on a beach that has trees or other shade producers, of course, but it will keep you and yours moving as you run from shady spot to shady spot.

◐ Make a towel tent. All you have to do is show your children how to make a simple tent by inserting sticks or driftwood into the sand and then draping towels over the tops of the sticks. As they crawl around underneath and make adjustments here and there, your children will be learning beginning engineering skills—and staying out of the sun.

◐ Hunt for buried treasure. You'll need to prepare for this activity at home, but it's worth it. Digging for buried treasure keeps everyone from toddlers to preteens busy for hours at the beach. All you need to do is cover a dozen shells or small rocks with gold or silver spray paint before

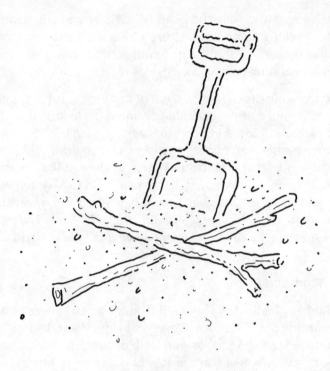

you go to the beach. When you get there, tell your child to close his eyes while you quickly bury the "treasure" in the sand, marking the spot with an X of sticks or a vertical stick. Then let him uncover his buried treasure. He'll want to do this again and again, also burying the treasure for you, and then having you bury it again for him to find. Of course, don't play this game with a child who is still inclined to mouth—and swallow—the golden booty.

◐ Take home sand on purpose. This activity starts at the beach and ends in your kitchen. It's a great way to extend your beach experience with a morning activity at home that involves making a clay that feels like wet sand and that molds like what you'd find at the beach as well. Collect two cups of the cleanest sand you can find, then sift it through a strainer to get out the odd stick, shell, or stone. Back at home, combine the sand with a cup of cornstarch, and let your child mix the two up. Add about one and a half cups of hot water and stir again, then take the mixture out of your child's hands while you cook it over low heat until it thickens. Once it is thick, pour it out onto a newspaper, let it cool for a moment, and after you test the temperature with your hands, let your child mold the warm, wet sand into whatever she likes. You can make her creations permanent by letting them harden for a day or two, or keep them for later play in a covered container.

WHAT TO DO WHEN YOU GO TO . . .

The Snow

To your child, the snow turns the whole world into the equivalent of a giant sandbox, with snow everywhere to pack and mold and stomp. Of course, there are some marked and obvious differences between playing with sand and snow, but many of the same activities can be performed with both substances. Why not build a snow castle? Or, for that matter, a sandman?

Naturally, you need to dress children warmly for outdoor play in the winter—but don't bundle them up so tightly that they cannot move with ease. In order to dress children appropriately for the weather, you will need to consider their activity level: A very active child can wear less, but one long ride on the sled and he'll quickly get cold.

Keep a child who will be out in the snow in waterproof outer layers, and always be sure to bring additional layers of clothing, as well as extra mittens, when you are venturing out in winter any distance from home. Wet, cold fingers become unbearable for everyone very quickly. Likewise, always bring some sort of alternative over-snow transportation, even if your toddler always insists on walking. There's nothing worse than having to carry a crying, wet, cold child home while you trudge through the snow.

And while your child plays outdoors, even if it is on your back porch, keep your eye (and your hands) on his face and other exposed skin to make sure it isn't cold. And enforce regular indoor breaks, where you can check the dampness of his clothing and his overall warmth.

MAKE A SNOW BOX

Suggested Ages: One year and up

Your Child's Special Skills and Interests: Sitting up, digging around

Preparation Time: 20 minutes

Materials: Plastic tub or baby bath; plastic spoons, knives, and cups

Why to try it: If you live in a place where you don't typically get a lot of snow, let your toddler have fun with the white stuff you do have. Corral the cleanest snow you can find, and load it into a plastic tub. A "snow box" like this can even be useful in snowy climates: Putting the snow in one place makes it more manageable, accessible, and enticing for babies, who, when

presented with the tub, know immediately to dig right in. It
also makes it easier for parents, who can move the box indoors,
where they don't have to worry so much about tiny little fingers getting too cold.

How to do it: Bring the tub into the garage if it is too cold
outside, and let your child play there or in the kitchen, placing
a towel underneath the box to soak up the mess. (If the weather
outside is mild, you can also play there, of course.) Once you
are set up, suggest the following activities: They can be done
using the snow box or out in the yard.

One Year and Up, Sometimes Younger

◐ Cookie cutters, cups, and plastic knives or spatulas are great snow toys for a one-year-old and up, or for an even younger child. She'll love imprinting the snow with the cookie cutters, then slicing and smashing it up with a plastic knife.

◐ Year-old children will enjoy simply digging in the snow with plastic spoons and measuring cups (bury some plastic toys for them to discover, for a special treat), whereas near-three-year-olds might enjoy making tiny snowmen, digging roads, or making snow houses. Children especially like this if you provide them with props—such as plastic cars, people, animals, and so forth.

◐ Provide your year-old baby or two-year-old toddler with a paintbrush and some washable paints, as well as a plastic knife or spoon to smash up the snow. He'll love painting the snow and mixing up the colors.

Two Years and Up

◐ A two-year-old will get a kick out of playing snow golf: Bury plastic cups in the snow in the yard so that their tops are flush with the top of the snow. Using a child-size broom as a "club," she can roll the balls across the snow into the cups.

TAKE A WINTER SNOW WALK

Suggested Ages: One year and up
Your Child's Special Skills and Interests: Walking outdoors
Preparation Time: 10 minutes to gather supplies

Materials: Food coloring, spray bottles; black paper, sled with a long rope for towing comfortably by parents

How to do it: If you are nervous about taking a young child out in the cold, remember: Babies are raised in such climates all over the far north, and their mothers don't keep them inside nine months a year. Go out and take a walk. If your child can't walk the whole way, bring a sled to pull along—the experience of being pulled in a sled is different enough to make even near-three-year-olds who have rejected the stroller hop right in. Plus, you need a fast escape vehicle if your child does get cold and you need to bring him home in a hurry. To make pulling a sled easier, always make sure the tow rope is adequately long so you won't have to hunch over to pull it. You can also customize it in any number of ways to increase the comfort factor. Use a dog leash to clip it onto the back belt loop of your pants or the jog stroller you are pushing for no-hand pulling, or slip a long stick through the loop in the rope and pull it with both hands with equal force. However you decide to move along, try some of the following activities as you go.

One Year and Up

◑ Catch a snowflake or two. Bring along a piece of black or other dark-colored construction paper on your walk. Hold the paper out to catch snowflakes in a light, dry snowstorm. You and your child of one year or so should clearly be able to see the delicate shape of the flakes. And when your paper gets too wet, show your child how to catch snowflakes the old-fashioned way: on her tongue.

◑ Stomp shapes in the snow. As soon as your child can walk, at around one year or so, he'll love to stomp down the snow. As he gets older, you can encourage him to give purpose to his stomping. Challenge him to stomp out a circle

or a square. This seemingly mindless task is absolutely con-
suming for toddlers, many of whom will keep stomping
long after the snow is as flat as the ground below it.

Two Years and Up

❍ Make yellow—and blue and green—snow. Add food coloring to a spray bottle filled with water until the water is
deeply colored. Then take your spray bottle along to color
your white world. A child of around two can usually spray
the snow herself, but even younger children will enjoy
watching you spray the snow. While you walk, leave a trail
of where you've been. When it is time to turn around and
head home, lure the still-wanting-to-walk child back by
telling her she can follow the color trail.

◐ Watch the snow melt. Right after the snow falls and the sun comes out, pick up handfuls of the lightest flakes you can find, and deposit them on a wood or metal surface. Within seconds they will virtually disappear. To any two- or three-year-old—and to some younger children—this is positively magic.

◐ Save a snowball or two. Pack away a few snowballs in the depths of your freezer to pull out next July. They'll be ice-balls by then, but still exciting to watch melt on the hot cement—and then cool (literally speaking) to step into.

WHAT TO DO WHEN YOU GO TO . . .

The Restaurant

You know you probably can't take your young child into restaurants with candles on the table (although some little babies will do fine sleeping in the dim light), but this doesn't mean you are condemned to a foreseeable future of eating out at establishments where you pick up the food at the counter and unwrap it at your table. If you are going to happily eat out at a restaurant somewhere in between fancy and takeout, keep in mind the following:

◐ Try to eat out when your child is either reasonably well rested or almost certain to sleep.

◐ Order immediately upon arrival if you have a toddler in

tow and ask for your child's food to be brought as soon as it is ready, regardless of the status of your own food.

◐ Specify that your child's drink be served in the smallest glass in the house, and then only three-fourths or one-half full, thus minimizing spill mess. Of course, the fates being what they are, children rarely knock over half-full glasses, only those that are filled to the brim and extra-large.

◐ Bring some pre-meal snacks that take a long time to eat: fruit leather that needs to be peeled, piece by piece, from the plastic; a container of O-shaped cereal to be picked up piece by piece; string cheese that can be eaten strip by strip; licorice sticks to be used as drinking straws.

◐ Always have travel-size packs of baby wipes for hands and faces, both yours and your child's, as well as for messes on the restaurant's high chair.

◐ If you can eat outside, do. For parents who spend a lot of their life picking up small pieces of food from their own floors at home, and then find themselves crawling under restaurant booths to do the same thing, dining al fresco is a fabulous alternative. Your baby will enjoy the increased activity outside, and the local birds and squirrels can handle at least some of the cleanup.

◐ Scan the restaurant for the best seat, in a young child's opinion. If you've got an infant in tow, for example, ask for a seat under a ceiling fan, if possible. As he lies back and looks at the ceiling, this might just be the best view in the house as far as he is concerned. If you have a toddler, you might ask for a seat that gives you a view of the kitchen. It may not be the best seat for adults, but your child will love seeing the kitchen door open and close and the huge trays of food come out. Balloons, fountains, and windows onto the street are also distracting and fun for young diners.

◐ Leave a big tip at any restaurant that seems particularly family friendly, and for any wait-staff that meets your sometimes odd requests with expedience. Who knows? You might want to become a regular. Be sure you'll get the same service next time, by acknowledging verbally and with a gratuity the extra work involved in serving a family.

◐ Come prepared with some quiet, tabletop activities that allow you to talk somewhat uninterrupted to other adults and that neither make a huge mess nor disturb other diners. Such activities might include the following.

Six Months and Up

◐ Another napkin, please. Lay a napkin flat on the table and have your fork wiggle underneath it toward baby—much to her delight. Or hold the napkin up in the air and drop it over your table, for baby to watch fall down slowly through the air. Arranging to have the napkin land on your head or your child's sets up a game of Napkin Peek-a-boo, which is another natural hit with babies.

◐ Shaker-cup hide-away. Cover the salt or pepper shaker with an empty paper or plastic cup. Move the cup/shaker all around the table, then lift it up to reveal, like magic, the shaker.

One Year and Up

◐ Consider the fun you have on you. You have more toys for your child in your possession than you might think. Consider the possibilities for a mirrored compact (look in it, use it to send reflected light around the room); a handful of credit cards (keep track of how many you have handed him); a set of bangle bracelets to wear and share; even a scrunchie pony tail holder, which will delight baby when put around his wrist.

◐ Play with spoons. At around a year and a half, your child will be happily occupied by the task of transferring water, one spoonful at a time, from one small half-full plastic or paper cup to another, empty one. Babies of this age also like performing those paper absorption tests that you see on television: Putting spoonfuls of water on paper napkins to watch them "disappear." And although this is messier than the cup activity, comparatively speaking, both are relatively clean (it's just water, after all). And it is a very quiet, literally absorbing game. Just ask for two cups and extra napkins.

Two Years and Up

◐ The cup's up. No one in the restaurant will mind if you quiet a starving two-year-old with this on-the-go construction activity. Grab or request a half-dozen paper cups. Now challenge your child to see how high she can stack a pyramid of the cups placed upside down. Next, turn the cups up. Work with your child to see how this makes the cups more difficult to stack. Then put a layer of straws over the open tops. Show her how closing off the openings gives you new ways to build. Once you've exhausted the possibilities with straws and cups (and if your food still hasn't arrived), look around the table for other possible props. What about a paper napkin on top to make a tent?

◐ Sugar packet sort. Grab a handful of sugar packets and sugar substitutes. Hand them to your child (who needs to have stopped putting things in her mouth), and show her

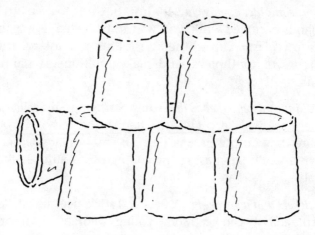

how to sort them by color, lay them out in different shapes, and stack them up.

◐ Coffee creamer crash. Don't let those tiny packages of liquid coffee creamer go to waste. Turn them into blocks, letting your child stack them up and then, of course, knock them over.

Two to Three Years and Up

◐ Table art.   Keep a lunch box full of simple art supplies in the car to be pulled out for restaurant use when the three broken crayons the restaurant provides prove less than compelling. If you have more than one child, a kit for each may be necessary, but the contents can be the same. The following activities will amuse a child of almost any age.

Three or four washable markers, a small drawing pad, and a paintbrush: Let the kids color with them. Then extend the activity by letting them turn their drawings into dreamy "watercolor" paintings by smearing over the top with a paintbrush dampened with water.

One container of play clay: It's just the thing to keep little hands occupied while you wait to be seated. Bring an empty plastic cup to use as a rolling pin, ask for stir straws or toothpicks, and make multi-media sculptures.

A film canister of beads and string: Stringing a bracelet or necklace will keep children happy and busy, but be sure they do the project over an empty plate. Otherwise, you'll be chasing the rolling beads all over the table.

Stickers and a sticker book: Peel and stick, peel and stick. This activity can keep some young children's attention for what would seem to be a mind-numbing amount of time.

A washable paint palette: If you are particularly adventurous, try this: It's not as messy as it sounds. Pull the plastic palette containing the tablets of washable watercolor paint out of the plastic-hinged case and stick it in a plastic bag, along with a handful of ear swabs. With a paper cup of water from the restaurant, your child can paint as easily as he can draw by dipping the swabs in the water to use as paintbrushes.

❧ It's a number's game. With just a set of dice you can play games right through the soup course with minimal mess. Write numbers from one to six on a piece of paper. Now simply take turns throwing the dice and keeping track of how many times each number comes up. And rather than haggling over one more bite, let the dice make the call. Agree to take as many more bites as a throw of the dice dictates. You can also play this with a bag of soup crackers, each eating just as many crackers as the number of the dice says.

◐ Have a silly contest. Balance a package of crackers on two
fingers. See who can talk the quietest, tear a shape from a
paper napkin, or catch you when you make a mistake saying the alphabet or counting. If there's anything that three-
year-olds love, it's a challenge with a bit of competition
thrown in to spice it up.

WHAT TO DO WHEN YOU GO ON . . .

The Walk

Whether you walk around the neighborhood or head to a local
park, a daily walk is a wonderful year-round habit to get into
when you have a young child in the home; this is an outing
that can be worked into the busiest schedules. The zoo may
not open until 10:00, the mall may close at 5:00 on weekends.
But you can take a walk at any time of the day. The early morning, when your child may already have you up before the rest
of the world, is a great time, as are the dusk hours. As the sun
sinks, you can reconnect quietly with your child and even enjoy a picnic sandwich dinner as you walk along.

   Whenever you choose to walk, you'll find the fresh air is
both invigorating for you and ultimately exhausting for your
child. The trip outside offers not only exercise for you both (if
she's walking), it also offers a true adventure. Wherever you
walk, you'll be exposing your child to the rhythms of the
world: She'll see the moon still up from the night before or just
rising in the evening. She'll experience wind, sun, and even

rain. She'll see the clouds and how they move. And then there is the ground below her feet. From picking up a feather to kicking a tin can, the ground is every bit as full of wonders as the sky. For urban walkers, many of these natural sensations still exist, but are supplemented with people-watching, the excitement of the noisy garbage truck, the animated window display, the flashing lights, the yummy smells of the bakery around the corner. With so much to take in, it's no wonder that walks with a young child are rarely brisk.

Indeed, walking with a young child is a stop-and-go experience, with the slow pace of looking and investigating easily lengthening a 20-minute route into an hour or more. Try to take your walks when you have plenty of time to linger over tiny flowers growing in sidewalk cracks, to practice balancing on landscaping railroad ties, or counting steps over and over again. As you develop your walk route, some of these regular sights will actually inspire your child to keep moving. Once you've peered through the underground tunnel running beneath your neighbor's driveway, remind your child of the flowers you always pet in the yard two houses away. Once you've stroked the flowers, the bridge where you drop sticks into the water is just around the corner. In this leap-frog manner, you'll be able to see, touch, and smell the sights but still keep some forward momentum going.

When you set out, always bring an alternative method of transportation (a backpack, stroller, tricycle with push bar, or wagon), even if your child is an insistent walker. You never know when she might completely break down in a tantrum and you will need to get home in a hurry. You'll also want to bring all of your regular going-out supplies, making sure to include water, a snack, sunscreen, a book or a toy, and an extra diaper and change of clothes. For ease of getting ready, it sometimes helps to keep all of these things packed in your stroller or backpack. And while the walk itself will offer plenty of entertainment for you and your child, you can always add interest to your routine with the following walk activities.

Six Months and Up

◐ Collect natural entertainment for your baby. As you walk along with baby in the pack or stroller, keep your eyes open for things to pick up and show him (being sure to keep a hand on the items yourself so baby doesn't pop them into his mouth, of course). Let baby feel a fuzzy leaf, a smooth river rock, a bumpy stick. As you present your passenger with these treasures, be sure to give him the words that describe what you are showing him. Before long, you'll be hearing them back.

◐ Sit down and look at the sky and the leaves. Find a quiet spot along your route where you can sit with baby in your lap and look up at the clouds and the rustling leaves and feel the sun and the wind. These kinds of moments will be at once exciting and soothing to many young children, especially if they are seeing these things for the first time. But don't stop after once or twice: Children enjoy these moments long after they've started school.

One Year and Up

◐ Be a natural crafts collector. You can turn many of your child's found treasures into crafts. Keep a bucket by your back door where you can toss the odd stick and stone, and a piece of floral foam to stick long pieces of wild grasses, dried seed pods, and so forth. The following three best ways to use this collection when it becomes overwhelming can be used with your baby or toddler as well as an older sibling:

1. A one-year-old is happy to turn the rocks he brings home into a set of natural blocks. Pull out the small and flat ones to show him how to build with them.
2. An 18-month-old will be delighted to make paper-

weight after paperweight. Just hand him a rock and a paintbrush and he'll be on his way.

3. A two- or three-year-old will enjoy trying to build the three little piggies' houses. You can use play dough as the mortar for a stone house and anchor a house of straw or sticks in a Styrofoam foundation.

◑ Prepare for a puddle stomp or an ice break. If it has been at all wet outside, be sure to bring or have your child wear her waterproof boots. As soon as your child can walk, she'll want to stomp in puddles. If you find watching this pursuit too tedious, wear your own wet-weather gear and stomp alongside her. Then see how long your wet shoeprints last on the cement, and have a contest to see whose two-footed jump can make the biggest splash. You can sail dandelion flowers atop the puddles, and make splashes throwing in small stones. In any case, you'll want to shorten your route on a puddle-filled day: You are sure to have many stops

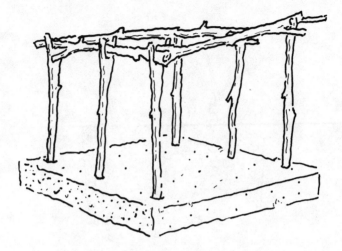

ahead. And don't forget the fun of the cold-weather version of this activity: stepping on frozen shallow puddles.
The sound and sight of the crack is an irresistible reward
to young children. And when you pick up the sheets of ice
and hold them up for your child to look through, or throw
them down for her to see them shatter, the thrill will continue. It also gives you an opportunity to start educating
your child early about why, when she sees that there is
water below, she wouldn't want to walk on ice that wasn't
over a shallow puddle.

Eighteen Months and Up

◗ Make a collector's basket. Turn an old berry basket into a
toy by stringing yarn through a hole on each side to make
a handle and then lining it with foil to keep the tiny treasures from falling through the holes. With this in hand, you
and your child can collect all sorts of fabulous booty:

leaves, rocks, sticks, and the occasional gum wrapper, among them.

❍ Let your child push the empty stroller. At this highly imitative time in your child's life, the chance to push the stroller like you do is a thrill. Depending on how easy your stroller is for a young child to push, this activity can also keep the momentum up during your walk. When you reach a small uphill incline, inform your child that she is actually pushing a trained stroller. Show her how she can push it a little ways and then release her grip. The stroller will go a little ways forward and then, to her delight, come rolling back. This demonstration of gravity at work is a thrill for your child. Just make sure you don't try it on a steep incline, and be on hand with your child to "catch" the returning stroller.

Two Years and Up

◐ Take a color walk. When your child begins to show an interest in and is starting to identify colors, you can reinforce this learning with a color walk. Bring along several envelopes, each with a different color of construction paper pasted on the front. As you walk, look for and collect samples of each color. While you are walking, you'll find you are both more observant than ever with this shared goal in mind, and when you return home, you can use your collected colors to make a color collage: Just put a couple of pieces of double-sided sticky tape on a piece of paper and let your child attach her finds.

◐ Bring along a bug catcher. Caterpillars in fall, worms after a rain, grasshoppers on a hot summer day: All of these crawling creatures are guaranteed to cross your child's path and will certainly warrant closer inspection by your young natural scientist. Try not to introduce your own fears or prejudices about the insects to your child, and discuss the amazing things about the bug she's looking at as calmly as you can. She will want to touch. Without making her afraid, let her know some bugs do sting, so it is best to handle them with a stick or net or to put them in a plastic jar to study them more carefully. Just be sure to bring along a net and a jar and then to let the bug go after you and your child have carefully studied it through the safe clear plastic.

◐ Wash your rocks. When you return home with a pocketful (or two) of rocks that your child has picked up, extend the activity by providing your young collector with a bowl of clean, soapy water, a bowl of clean warm water, an old toothbrush, and a towel. Then let your rock hound clean off his finds. This is a thoroughly absorbing and rewarding activity for most two- and three-year-olds, who will thrill

to what their efforts uncover, even if it still looks like an old brown rock to you.

 Take a chalk walk. Like Hansel and Gretel, you and your child can leave marks along your route. Only, unlike these storybook characters, yours won't be eaten up, letting you follow them all the way back home. Bring along several pieces of sidewalk chalk. As you walk, take the time to draw a letter here or there, or to trace the outline of a hand, foot—even your child's entire body. Some kids will want to stay and keep drawing; remind them that they are making a "trail." The return home will be easier to inspire: They'll happily hurry along to see the tracks they left behind.

WHAT TO DO WHEN
YOU GO TO . . .

The Playground

In some ways, the playground may seem to be the least demanding of outings, at least as far as parents are concerned. After all, there's no having to set up play dates—some playmates are probably already there—as are the toys, in the form of swing sets and slides, jungle gyms, and teeter totters. But like most outings, if your young child is really to get the most out of the experience, your participation is essential. To start with, for instance, he needs your help in learning the laws of the playground.

While older kids certainly know the score on playground etiquette, including exactly how to get a shot on the swing or go down the slide, most kids under three lack these more advanced social skills. Left to their own devices, other kids can be brutal teachers of these lessons, regardless of how little your child is in comparison to them. You will be needed to help your child gently get in line, and you may have to go down the slide along with him to ensure that he gets off in ample time before the next child comes barreling down.

Don't feel uncomfortable playing alongside your child at the playground, as long as you don't get on equipment that is not designed for your weight. Your child will relish the experience of playing with you, and eventually you will look back and treasure it as well. Remember: It won't be long before your child won't need or even want you as his playground playmate. Playing with your child also puts you in the right place to prevent playground injuries—a very real concern. Stand close to where your child is playing and keep a careful eye on him. Annually, more than 200,000 children are treated for playground-equipment-related injuries, with more than 70 percent of these involving falls off the equipment to the ground below. It's just smart to be standing where you can do some catching.

Playing with your child at the playground also gives you opportunities for teaching your child all sorts of concepts that would be more difficult at home, and gets you both fresh air and exercise. Even for children under one, the playground offers an exciting and different view of their favorite subject—other kids—while letting you gaze on your not-so-distant future in wonderment. Yes, in a year or so, your baby will be like the kids you see. With baby strapped into a front carrier, you can also ride the teeter totter or swing slowly in a swing, much to a six-month-old's delight. While you play with your toddler, walk around with your baby, or keep an eye on an older sibling off on the merry-go-round, consider the following playground games.

One Year and Up

◐ What goes up . . . Bring along a small soft ball and let your child play catch with the slide. Show her how to roll it down the slide a few times. Once she gets the hang of it, show her how to stand at the bottom and catch the rolling ball, and then roll it back up so that it can come back down again.

◐ Silly swing. Once your child is old enough to sit in a swing alone (which can happen early, if your playground has toddler swings), play this silly game while you swing: As your child swings toward you, put out your hands and tell her in a mock serious voice to "go away," pushing her back.

Of course, within seconds, she'll be back again, giggling the whole time that she has "disobeyed" you. You can also pretend that she is chasing you. Push her away and say, "Now, don't follow me." Begin to walk away and then turn around to see her coming back at you again. When you pretend-lecture her to stop following you, she'll find you absolutely hilarious.

Two Years and Up

○ Practice directions. Because so much movement is involved in playground equipment, the experience offers parents a great time to work with directional prepositions with their children. Repeat the words "up, down, up, down" as you ride the teeter totter. Hold onto metal poles with both hands and swing "around and around." Talk about going under and over different pieces of playground equipment.

🜄 Follow the Leader. This age-old game is a great way to introduce your child to all aspects of the playground. Take turns being the leader and climbing under and over the slide, moving in between the vacant swings, balancing on the logs that enclose the playground, making big jump tracks in the sand for each other to match.

Three Years and Up

🜄 Count on it. For a child near three, the playground offers all sorts of activities to practice counting skills. He will enjoy going up on the teeter totter ten times, swinging to you five times, or counting the steps up the slide every single time. Once he has reached the top of his counting ability (whether that is 5, 10, or 20), let him start over again and count up his teeter tot bumps once more.

🜄 Do "tricks." Near-preschool-age children revel in their great new control over their bodies and love to invent new tricks to show off their skills. You can help them expand their capabilities while teaching them what is and isn't safe by staying close by their side as they show you new "tricks," such as going down the slide with one knee bent, turning their heads from side to side as they swing back and forth, or climbing up on the gym and waving with one hand. When they propose things that won't work or could be dangerous, you can explain why and suggest alternatives, as well as stand close by to spot your child and prevent an injury. Older siblings will also often want to join in, with a performance of their much more advanced feats. Naturally, the same cautions apply.

WHAT TO DO WHEN YOU GO TO . . .

The Store

All you want is a gallon of milk and some bread and bananas. The very fact that your needs are so simple and the outing should be so quick and easy seems to inspire contrary behaviors in some young children. Call it the law of parental expectations: The minute children sense you are rushing them along and their little needs and preferences are not being taken seriously into account, that's the minute their little heels dig in. No getting in the car seat. No getting out of the car seat. And no going into the grocery store.

Of course, this doesn't happen all the time, but it happens enough to make some parents begin to fear the simplest errands if they have to bring their baby along. Your approach to this situation will naturally depend on you and your child's personalities. But nearly any bad attitude (yours or your child's) can be at least somewhat improved by the possibility of some fun for both parties. This doesn't necessarily mean that lots of extra time for shopping is necessary. Many in-store activities can be quick; some can even help you get your errands done more swiftly, especially if you turn them into a race or game with a two-and-a-half-year-old. Just talking to your child and including her in the process of shopping is often enough. And because much of the time that busy parents spend with their children does occur when they are running errands, it just makes sense to try to turn the time into a quality experience.

Furthermore, although it may seem easier just to get your business done and hope your child will be patient, this approach isn't always effective and can even be unsafe. You need to pay close attention to your child in the store, and not just because you don't want her taking down a display methodically while you are comparing prices at the other end of the aisle. Literally tens of thousands of children under age five are treated in emergency rooms for injuries in the grocery store, most associated with falling from their seat in the shopping cart. If your child is riding in the cart, it's important that she be strapped in with the provided belt, and that you stay relatively close.

Six Months and Up

◑ Name your food. Of course, other shoppers may glance over to see who you are talking to, and baby, reclining in an infant seat on your shopping cart, may not seem to pay attention. But this lively patter will keep baby feeling happy and included and will develop her language skills, even if they aren't immediately evident. You will also thrill any young child if you take a trip by the floral section to smell the flowers, or let her feel the cool cucumber on her cheek before you put it in the basket.

Eighteen Months and Up

◑ A cart of her own. Plastic, child-size grocery carts are available at most toy and discount stores. Or use one of your child's earlier walker toys, now renamed "grocery cart." Whatever you use, most almost-two-year-olds will delight at the chance to push their cart alongside yours and may even pick up various items and put them in their cart at your request. Simply keep the cart in the car at all times so you'll be ready to go shopping together at a moment's notice, and be sure to check what is in your child's cart before you are first in line at the checkout. You might be surprised at its contents (and want to put some of them back!).

◐ Hold the list. Keeping the real list with you, give your child another shopping list (any piece of paper with writing will do). Tell your child that he has the shopping list and is helping you by giving it to you whenever you request it (which may need to be often). You might also give your child a small change purse (if he's no longer in the habit of putting coins in his mouth, anyway) so that he can provide you with extra change as needed. Both of these tasks make your child a participant and give him the feeling that he is a needed help.

Two Years and Up

◐ Red light, green light. If you've got the time, let your child be the boss of your grocery store cruising. When he says "green light," you go; when he says "red light," you stop. Of course, if he's saying go when you really need to stop, you might declare an imaginary traffic jam is ahead and insist that you stop just long enough for you to reach over and grab a can or two of tomatoes. You can also tell him what you are looking for and let him scan the aisles as you go along, shouting "red light" when he spots the needed item.

◐ Make your child your partner. Enlist your child's help even before you go to the store. Ask her what to put on your shopping list, and let her make a shopping list of her own. Once you get to the store, let her pull her favorite cereal off the shelf and put it in the basket, or pick out three good apples for school. And make a habit of shopping by number, color, and letter. As you cruise the aisles with a walking toddler, periodically send her on missions you know she can achieve. Ask her to get the blue box with the letter "O" on the outside; or the yellow jar with the red label. As long as the items are close and at eye level, pulling them off the shelf should be an exciting but possible goal. If you are traveling with a baby or toddler and an older sibling, making your older child feel like a real partner is especially important, since you really will probably need his or her assistance.

Three Years and Up

◐ Draw your dinner. Make up a shopping list just for your child to use, no reading necessary. Even those with limited artistic ability can draw the shape of bananas, a pear, corn on the cob, a popsicle, a stick of butter, and so forth. Limit your child's list to a half dozen things you can draw, and write the more difficult items on your own. When you go to the store, your child can "help" you by reminding you of items on his list and even fetch them himself as you make your rounds.

Chapter Seven

~~~~~~~~

TRAVEL AND COMMUTE

Fun on the Road and in the Air

You have to get from here to there, and many times, your child has to accompany you. While some children love to go, for others, the car seat is a prison—a place where they are both confined and separated from the ones they love in the Siberia of the backseat (or equally bad—the strapped-down airplane seat directly beside you). Like many prisoners, your child will often be inclined to yell for freedom, often pitching a few toys into the front seat, struggling to get out, and screaming at his jailer to make their point.

How do you cope with an unhappy traveler? First, never give in to demands that compromise your child's safety. He must stay in the car seat or in his buckled-down airplane seat. Properly used and installed, car seats reduce automobile fatalities in infants by 71 percent; in toddlers by 54 percent. And airplane flight attendants simply won't allow you to be up and walking when the sign indicates you need to be seated. Young auto travelers must also stay in the backseat. This reduces car fatalities by an estimated 36 percent. In fact, child safety experts recommend that all children ride in the backseat until the age of 12. If you have older children, keeping them in the back can either help or hinder the ease of traveling with a toddler or baby, depending on their attitude. Nonetheless, the backseat is where they should be.

Once you've ensured your child's safety, the most you can do for the consistently unhappy traveler is limit his travel. Do errands without him if you can, and always plan car or airplane trips for his happiest (or sleepiest, if it is a long trip) time of day. You should also schedule plenty of time for all of your jaunts out if you can—there is nothing worse than trying to rush an already angry child.

And when your child needs or has to be with you, try to make it as fun as possible for you both by employing the following games, activities, and travel toys. Once he starts to enjoy his seat-belted "prison," the bars might just crumble down.

WHAT TO DO WHEN YOU TRAVEL . . .

By Airplane

You can't leave your baby, your luggage, or your car unattended. You have to haul your car seat—with your child—from distant parking lots, since your baby can't ride in the car without it. You have to wait in lines, locate and pull various pieces of paper out upon request, and stumble through security. The only good thing about air travel with a child under two, it sometimes seems, is that at least you don't have to pay extra for all of this agony.

On the other hand, going through all of this alone with your child (or even with your child and a friend or partner) is something of a bonding experience, even if your child is still a very young baby. Because you often need to attend to your child rather constantly to keep him from disturbing others on the plane, you have chances to really talk and play with him that you might otherwise have missed. If your partner is your traveling companion, you are also able to practice a whole day of shared parenting. If you have older children along as well, they will likely see how much their help is needed and be a real partner and companion to you, at least until they get tired too. Be sure to pay close attention to their needs as much as you can.

You are also on what might qualify as your first family adventure, with all the good and bad that entails. After all, during a long day's travel you are overcoming obstacles together and figuring out what works for all of you. In some ways, this challenge is rewarding. If nothing else, it does make you appreciate how truly unhassled your pre-child air travel was. A long layover? By *themselves?* What are these solo adult travelers complaining about?

Of course, there are ways to at least slightly lessen the stress factors involved in air travel with baby. For example, you might try the following:

◗ Bring, rent, or borrow a backpack or front pack if your baby or toddler enjoys these conveyances. Most have storage for diapers and bottles built in (so there is no need for a diaper bag) and, combined with a fanny pack carried in front of your waist for tickets, cash, teething biscuits, and tissue, provide relatively hands-freed movement through the airport.

◐ Carry plastic spoons, napkins, and throw-away bibs in easy-to-reach places.

◐ Take advantage of toddler treats the airport provides: moving sidewalks to stand on, water fountains to drink from, airport "trains" to ride, window views of airplanes taking off.

◐ Purchase healthy snacks you don't have to bring from home, even if you must pay extra. Yogurt, bagels, fruit, milk, and cereal are almost always available in airport snack shops.

◐ Try to carry as little as possible onto the plane. You have enough to manage with just your child, your wallet, your tickets, your child carrier, and your absolute essentials, like diapers. And since you won't be able to travel without checking anything anyway, why not check everything you can? Your arms and back will be glad you did, not to mention the person waiting in the aisle behind you who would have had to wait while you tried to stow it all away.

◐ Seek refuge where you can—and pay for it if necessary. If you will be doing a lot of plane travel with your child under three, these are the years to consider splurging on an airline club membership. Popular with business travelers, these clubs provide free juice and crackers, television (this is one of those acceptable times to indulge in watching it, if necessary), clean bathrooms with no lines, a safe place to put your luggage, and relative quiet. Some airports also have tiny concourse kiosks for rent, complete with televisions, soft couches, and telephones. If you have a long layover, consider these. It is also always worthwhile to stop at the airport information desk to see if the terminal has any special rooms or areas for children. These are not common, but they do exist, and are a boon to traveling parents and their children.

STAY SEATED FOR FUN

What to do when the seat belt light is flashing.

Suggested Ages: Birth to one year

Why to try it: The 20 minutes during takeoff and landing when the remain-in-your-seat light starts flashing is the equivalent of an in-transit arsenic hour for parents traveling with young children. The second your child has to stay seated, she will almost instinctively want to move. Right now. Or else. This is bad news whether your child is sitting in your lap (where she is likely to bop you in the nose) or in her car seat next to you. And believe it or not, you can take some comfort in knowing that it is worse news for you than for your traveling companions. Because no matter how much your child's behavior irritates them, it is your ears that are in direct proximity of the screaming.

How to do it: If you can get your child to be amused, or at least distracted, by each of the following activities for even three minutes, you'll be in the air—and back on the ground—in no time. Incidentally, these same activities work whenever you and your child are belted down side-by-side or you have to hold your child in your lap.

Three Months and Up

◐ Try a fun preposition. Begin teaching a baby—or reinforcing for a toddler—the concepts of direction, location, and space. Using a stuffed animal or any other object you can quickly put your hands on, begin moving the object into different locations as you narrate, "The book is *on* my head, *under* my arm, *over* my nose, *in* my mouth! Babies will find even these simple movements very amusing; for older children, a version of the game in which you say one thing and do another is a real hoot.

◐ Wear your toys. Think about what you wear on your travel day. Without carrying anything extra, you can bring along toys if you wear a shirt with pockets (to hide things in), a couple of jangling bracelets, and other interesting accessories to look at, play with, or touch, such as belts, necklaces, barrettes, watches, rings, and earrings. A wallet full of photographs can also be very helpful. What about one of those necklaces composed of bubble solution and a wand? It may look juvenile with the rest of your ensemble, but you won't be sorry to have worn it when you are stuck in Chicago for an extra hour.

◐ Make it an open-and-shut case. For baby or older child, this game combines teaching the concepts of "open" and "closed" with the fun of making silly faces and expressions. First, open everything you can think of, all at once: your eyes, mouth, arms, fingers, purse, magazine, overhead light. Now, close it all up again. You should be able to stretch this activity to last two minutes or even more.

Six Months and Up

◐ Give your baby a hearing checkup. Ask the flight attendant for a blanket. Using the blanket for cover, hide baby's rattle or other musical toy under the blanket in different locations (near your shoulder, on your lap, under your knees). Now, shake the rattle. Can baby lift up the blanket to find it? If you don't have a rattle, use an empty beverage can with a penny inside. But don't let baby hold this homemade rattle. The penny is a choking hazard.

◐ Which hand is it? Your moves may be obvious, but you'll still be David Copperfield to your baby or toddler as you

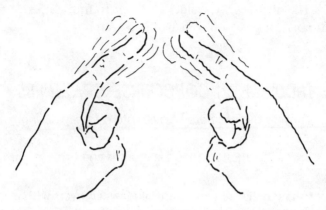

move a shiny or desirable object (a ring, coin, or piece of candy) back and forth between your hands and then ask him to guess or point to which clinched hand holds the treasure. If your baby is too young to guess, simply let him watch as you "guess" yourself.

Nine Months and Up

Put on a finger play. Balance baby on your knees, raise your hands with two index fingers pointed high, and put on a show with your fingers as undressed puppets who talk in squeaky or silly voices (especially important for babies). Wag, wiggle, and nod your fingers in turn as they animatedly discuss everything from how silly Mommy is to which of the two fingers is the tallest or the smartest. Young children find these pointless arguments absolutely hilarious.

One Year and Up

Play I Spy with a magazine. Grab an in-flight magazine and start scanning the page. Can your child find the yellow duck? The airplane? Ask older children to find colors, letters, or numbers or give you something to search for.

INDULGE IN CONCOURSE CRAZINESS
Turning a nightmare layover into a family outing.

Suggested Ages: Six months and up

Why to try it: From your point of view, layovers with a child in tow are different and much busier than what you may remember from your childless plane-trip days. You will need to take your child to the bathroom, get food and water, possibly change dirty clothes, and get ready at the gate for your next flight.

But once these things have been taken care of, consider your child's point of view. As far as she is concerned, air travel involves the following: First, you tie her down for two hours and confine her to a small space. Then you turn her loose in a building the size of multiple football fields and tell her to stay right beside you. Is it any wonder she finds this difficult?

Surviving layovers with a baby or toddler in tow requires creativity, energy—and a little cold hard cash. Pack like a pro and you'll still feel the need to buy a few surprises to occupy your child. Stash away a ten in an easy-to-reach pocket for these emergency buys. Even though airport shops are expensive, you'll still have plenty of change left if you handle your purchases creatively.

One commonsense caution for airport gift shops: If you have an adult traveling partner, leave your child with him or her while you quickly

go purchase a surprise and bring it back. Once a
child hits toddlerhood, bringing her into a
crowded airport gift shop is always a risky prop-
osition: You'll be looking at buying something
you didn't intend to, like the $10.95 souvenir shot
glass your daughter just knocked off the shelf.

Six Months and Up

○ Postcards: Buy two each of six postcards, then challenge
your toddler to match up the pairs. Once you tire of this
amusement, give half the cards to your child to pretend-
write letters home on, and take the other half for you to
actually write notes on. This is a parallel play that toddlers

really enjoy. For babies around six months who are actively exploring book hinges, an accordion set of postcards or a book of postcards is an inexpensive amusement that you can also use later, provided your child hasn't gummed them up too much.

◐ Key Chains: You might not give these a second look, but your baby will. Clip them onto a zipper for a toy that won't go under the seat. When you buy them, you'll want to examine them closely to make sure there are no parts baby can mouth or chew off and choke on.

◐ Balls: These are usually available in airport gift shops. Buy one and use it to roll between you and your toddler as you sit on the floor at the gate waiting for the next flight. Balls are also a great stranger-danger buster for toddlers, as they offer a way of "introducing" themselves to other nearby travelers, who are usually only too happy to have a diversion themselves.

One Year and Up

◐ Build a luggage fort. If there is no room to run and jump, pile up your luggage around your chair and make suitcase walls (no roof) you and your child can play in. Pick up some drinks and have a tea party within its confines.

◐ Push and pull yourself along. If you have to move from place to place, sometimes a pull or push toy can be a great motivator. Let your child pull or push for a while and then chase after you while you pull or push the toy. But don't introduce this game if you are in a real hurry. It gets you from place to place, but not quickly.

Eighteen Months and Up

◐ Play airport hopscotch. Look at the floor around your gate. If it's got a tile pattern built in (and most airports do) create a game in which you and your toddler hop from square to square, circle to circle. It's a great way to quickly burn off extra energy before you are strapped down again—just be sure your "hopscotch" area is quiet and removed from traffic flow.

◐ Do your nails. Sometimes trivial and untraditional activities make the best airport amusement. A pack of emery boards can keep some children busy filing their nails (and yours) on any number of takeoffs and landings. Bubble blowing and nail painting (with washable paint) are also fun amusements, and the supplies are usually available in gift stores.

WHAT TO DO WHEN YOU TRAVEL . . .

By Car

CARRY A SIX-PACK

Suggested Ages: Three months and up

Your Child's Special Skills and Interests: Needing to play in car

Preparation Time: 10 minutes

Messiness Quotient: Negative—this helps you deal with
the mess.

The Sibling Factor: Be sure to pack a six-pack for each child.

Materials: Empty cardboard six-pack holder, baby toys or
toddler toys

Commonsense Caution: Keep your eyes on the
road, even when you need to pass your child a
toy or cookie. And keep both hands on the wheel
while you drive. Try to pass things to baby only
when the car is stopped.

Why to try it: Simply taking all of baby's stuff in and out of
the car for each trip is a hassle. And then there's the problem
of finding what you need when you need it. You can't reach

deep into the diaper bag while you drive, nor is it easy to retrieve a rattle that has rolled off the seat and onto the floor. You need a tool that lets you grab what you need when you need it and take things back and forth to the car easily.

How to do it: Save a sturdy six-pack cardboard container to use in the car. You can stash baby's essentials in each separate compartment: teething biscuits in one, a rattle or pacifier in another, and travel wipes for you and baby in another. A typical baby travel kit might also include a small, child-safe mirror, a set of stacking cups, a tiny paperboard book, or other favorite plaything. A toddler kit might hold cassette tapes, small books or picture cards, a small spiral notebook, crayons and stickers, a sippy cup filled with water, and a few well-packaged snacks. If you have an even older child, let her have her own six-pack of fun for the car (packed by herself) as well.

After each trip, simply grab the handled pack with an extra finger (while you carry baby and the diaper bag with the rest) and later re-stock the food and rotate the toys to keep baby from getting bored on the next trip; leave essentials—like travel wipes—constantly replenished and in the pack. The ultimate beauty of this type of carrier becomes abundantly clear after a few trips: If things get spilled inside it, or the cardboard starts to wear out, turn the six-pack into a garbage carrier on its last trip out of the car and then throw the whole thing away. You can always start fresh with a new one.

CUSTOMIZE YOUR CAR

Suggested Ages: Three months and up

Your Child's Special Skills and Interests: Becoming bored with looking at the back of the backseat

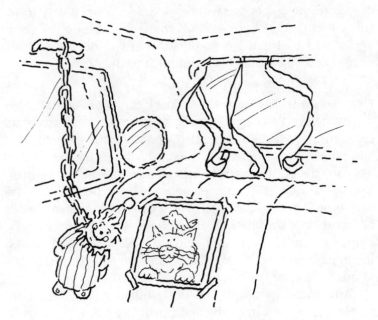

Preparation Time: 10 minutes

Messiness Quotient: Medium

The Sibling Factor: Many catalogs sell car-use trays, pillows, and toy storage systems for toddlers. Be sure to customize your older child's car space as well.

Materials: Child-safe mirror, bright large magazine pictures, tape, plastic rings, glass prisms or crystals, bells, bright ribbons

Commonsense Caution: Make sure whatever you put in the backseat with your children is safe for them to play with unsupervised and that all taped-on items are secure and pose no hazard to baby if he or she falls down. And decorations should, of course, never obstruct your view or attention as driver.

Why to try it: You'd get bored looking at your backseat up-holstery all the time, too.

How to do it: If you travel a lot with baby, make a habit of changing the scene for your backward-facing baby regularly. In addition to securely attaching a child-safe mirror within baby's view, consider tightly taping large, interesting magazine photographs onto the seat where baby can see them or onto the back of one of your window shades. Be creative as you decorate, thinking about ways to use movement, color, and light. Along the rear windows (far from baby's reach) tape a few brightly colored or shiny ribbons that will flutter in the air from the car or the open windows, or tape a few pieces of colored see-through plastic onto the glass for a rainbow effect. You can also tie a small crystal light catcher or prism to your rear-view mirror so that its colored light reflections will be thrown around the car. A set of jingle bells or light wind chimes is also a handy rearview mirror attraction that you can set a-ringing with just a wave of your hand. You can also fasten toys within baby's reach, using a set of plastic rings chained together with a toy on the end. This contraption can usually be secured to one of the handles above the backseat windows.

PLAN YOUR ROUTE

Suggested Ages: One year and up

Your Child's Special Skills and Interests: Sitting forward in car seat, looking out windows

Preparation Time: None

Messiness Quotient: None

Materials: None

The Sibling Factor: An older child can help point out these favorite sights along the route.

Why to try it: To give your child a sense of where you are and where you are going; to provide something for your child to look forward to while you drive.

How to do it: If there are certain trips you take every day, don't vary your route. Your child will enjoy the predictability of the same trip every day, especially because the passage of expected landmarks will allow him to mark time in the car. From the moment your child is able to see out the window, begin pointing out the sights. Things of great interest to your child will include silly billboards, flashing lights, any kind of animal, flowers, rocks, and buildings of interesting shapes and colors. The other advantage of a set route is that it allows you to alert baby well in advance of one of these landmarks. There is probably nothing worse—as far as your child is concerned—than to have things pointed out to him that you have already passed or will pass momentarily, leaving him looking around frantically while you explain that "it's back there."

LOOK AT THE SIGNS

Suggested Ages: One year and up

Your Child's Special Skills and Interests: Facing forward, looking out window, learning shapes and colors

Preparation: None

Messiness Quotient: None

Materials: None

The Sibling Factor: Give an older child more difficult word or letter challenges. See if she can find all the letters in the alphabet—in order—as you drive along.

Why to try it: Reinforce the shapes and colors your toddler is learning while you drive.

How to do it: As you drive, keep an eye on the road far ahead. When you see a shape or color that your child will recognize, ask him if he can see a yellow triangle or a white square. It's a simple challenge for you, a rewarding one for him. And it keeps both of you happily and safely engaged as you travel along.

HAVE A SILLY TALK

Suggested Ages: Two years and up

Your Child's Special Skills and Interests: Talking, developing a sense of humor

Preparation: None

Messiness Quotient: None

The Sibling Factor: Your older child will love to see you being silly.

Materials: None

Why to try it: Let's face it: As a conversation starter with your toddler, "How are you doing?" is often bound to fall about as flat as "How was preschool?" Make your banter lively with your toddler by hitting her where she lives: smack in the middle of the Ridiculous Zone.

How to do it: The time you spend driving does offer you an opportunity for talking, but many times this is easier if you aim for silly rather than sophisticated interchanges. For one thing, silly talk is easier for you to carry on while you are driving, and it is more likely to continue on its own. Announce that you are going to pick up bananas, blueberries, and . . . basketballs for breakfast. The joke will not be lost on your toddler, who is bound to want to contribute her own ridiculous list. You can use the same joke over and over: Tell your child you are going to the grocery, the gas station, and . . . the moon. Such conversation isn't only silly: It is also a serious learning tool, helping your child learn about groupings and logic and what does and doesn't go together.

Other ridiculous topics to use on your next commute:

- Try out funny sounds. "Wait, is that a zoober?" Any silly words, especially with the letters *z*, *s*, *j*, *g*, *p*, and *b* combined with double vowels, are bound to be entertaining.

- Make up funny rhymes. Just like the old song: "Anna Anna Bo Banna, Fe, Fi, Fo Fanna . . ."—humorous rhymes guarantee riots of laughter. At the same time, they reinforce language learning as your child hears new sounds and letter combinations.

- Practice silly storytelling. Ask your child for a subject for a story. He may pick something easy—like a rabbit. Or he may look around and pick the first thing he sees—like a stoplight. Then ask for something else. Your job, of course, is to quickly make up a story that has these two objects as its main characters, interacting in whatever way, however unlikely, you can think up while you drive.

PICK UP A FEW BROCHURES

Suggested Ages: One year and up

Your Child's Special Skills and Interests: Looking at pictures,
playing with paper

Preparation Time: None

Messiness Quotient: Medium to high

The Sibling Factor: An older sibling might be able to rip out
pictures he or she likes and paste them in a notebook (using
your in-car art kit supplies).

Materials: None

Why to try it: It's an easy and fun habit to get into that will
serve you well in family travel for years to come.

How to do it: As you leave the restaurant or the gas station,
make a habit of grabbing a couple of the business cards or bro-
chures that are often displayed in such places and handing
them to your child for "reading material." Because they often
fold out and have pictures of people and animals, your child
will find them exciting, and they may keep her amused for at
least part of the next leg of your journey.

MAKE A CAR-TRAVEL SURVIVAL KIT

Suggested Ages: One year and up

Your Child's Special Skills and Interests: Facing forward, amusing
self for periods of time

Preparation Time: 10 minutes

Messiness Quotient: Medium—you have to put thinks back inside after each trip.

Materials: Plastic lunchbox; special travel toys and supplies

The Sibling Factor: If you've got two kids, you need two travel kits.

> **Commonsense Caution:** Since you will be driving and unable to closely supervise, make sure all the items you put in your child's travel kit are safe and appropriate for his age, posing no choking or strangulation hazards.

Why to try it: Just as hiding house toys for a while can make them seem fresh when you bring them out again, keeping a kit in the car with toys that can only be used there gives them a certain attractiveness that will hold your child's attention for at least the first part of each car journey.

How to do it: Pack a hard-sided lunchbox with a variety of eye- and attention-catching treats that are appropriate for your child's current age and interests (you will have to change this box every few weeks or so), and give it a permanent place stashed under the car seat. Two possible versions, with suggested items, include:

Baby car kit: Squishy liquid-filled toys, balls that make noises or light when shaken, a silky scarf, a small board book, a hinged box that can be opened and closed.

Toddler car kit: Small coloring books or blank notepads or books (small enough to be laid flat against a car seat, knee, or thigh); small box or bag of crayons or colored pencils; small bag of treasures—a 6-inch piece of silky ribbon to pretend-tie, a dozen small used greeting cards or cut-out magazine pictures to look at, two small pretend stuffed or plastic animals or people, a small squeeze flashlight, a glue stick for impromptu tearing and pasting, pipe cleaners to twist and shape.

Chapter Eight

~~~~~~~~

SPECIAL EVENTS

Making Some Days More Special
Than Others

Special events are often as much about you as about your child—especially during your child's first year of life, when everyone will remind you that they won't remember anything you do anyway. Don't pay attention to them. Holidays and other special events can inspire you with new ways to teach your children, activities to try, and things to talk about. Which means that celebrating them—to whatever degree you wish—is hardly a waste.

Just as they do for you, holidays help your child mark the passage of time and create set reference points in memory. Your 18-month-old won't understand that something happened in June. But he might understand that it happened before his birthday, or after he got to go on the Easter egg hunt. Sooner than you think, these special, recurring dates will begin to help your child form the beginnings of knowledge of the months, the years, and the movement of time, as well as the cyclical rotation that allows these special events to repeat themselves again and again. These events will also punctuate and highlight the changing of the seasons, reinforcing the sense of change and movement of time their transitions naturally give.

The seasons themselves are worth marking with young children for exactly the same reasons. Like holidays, your celebration of a new season doesn't need to be grand or complicated. But using the change as a basis for conversation, decoration, games, activities, crafts, and even parties is a great way to introduce variety into the routine of the entire family.

Holidays and special events are also about the creation of new traditions for your young family. Four years may pass before your child appreciates the ornaments marking his early life that hang on your tree. It may be much longer before your child even understands that he had a birthday party when he turned one and that you made an imprint of his hands. But this lag in time between when you did things and when your child noticed that you'd done them has its own sweet rewards. For one thing, you will have had time to get some of your traditions down like clockwork. You'll have already made the homemade dreidel and the grass Easter basket a few times by the time your child wants to be a fully active participant. Even better, by the age of four or five, your child will look around and truly appreciate all of your efforts. He will ask you again and again about these early holidays. And you'll be able to talk (and provide actual evidence) about the things you've done and have always done for his entire life, even if that life has only been five years long. For your child, of course, this is his entire history. Knowing that some things have always happened can only help strengthen his sense of stability and belonging and make all of the holidays to come more special for everyone.

WHAT TO DO DURING . . .

THE WINTER HOLIDAYS

Maybe it is because they mark the shortest days of the year, when you are the most housebound. Or perhaps it is because they inspire nostalgia for your own childhood, or even the childhood you wished you had. Whatever the reason, the winter holidays are likely to inspire even the least domestic parents to get out the cookie cutters and the glitter.

And it is true that if you've always wanted to try out homemade holiday crafts and cooking but were shy about your own skills, having a young child in your home does give you the perfect excuse to try again. Even better, since the things you are making are also being made by a two- or three-year-old, a little imperfection is to be expected.

But whatever you do, don't force yourself into holiday projects with your child you are too busy to truly enjoy. If you do, you won't be making the kind of memories you are hoping for, regardless of what you end up creating. Give yourself plenty of time for even the simplest of projects, and keep all of your holiday expectations modest, so you have a chance of exceeding them. The perfect holiday with young children is most certainly the one with the least stress and the most time for you to be together.

Gift-giving, too, should be kept at low levels to keep the holiday from overwhelming and ultimately stressing out your child. If grandparents shower you with presents despite your protests, consider doling out the gifts one day at a time before the holidays so that they can truly be appreciated. And if grandparents and other fans of your children who send gifts aren't with you for the actual holiday, think about opening their gifts early, with them on the phone so they can hear your child's reaction (if he's old enough to react) so that your child will begin to realize who gave him the gift.

Remember that what you are trying to teach your child during the holidays isn't avarice or greed. As you think about gifts and talk to others about gifts for your child, remember that your child will be taking cues about holiday expectations from you. If you emphasize gifts and the excitement of opening them up, he will too. Try to connect the gifts with the giver in your child's mind, and to give gifts that are developmentally and personally appropriate for your child. For most young children, a box full of ribbons and feathers and scraps of silky fabric will be far more appreciated than the season's hot new toy or the latest movie tie-in product. And whenever the demands of the holiday begin to overtake— personally, socially, and financially—the joy of the season, remember that the thing your child wants most from you at the holidays is the same thing he wants all year: your relaxed time and attention.

MAKE YOUR OWN WRAPPING PAPER

Suggested Ages: 18 months and up

Your Child's Special Skills and Interests: Painting, printing

Preparation Time: 10 minutes

Messiness Quotient: Medium to high

The Sibling Factor: Older children will enjoy the cool factor of these activities despite their simple nature.

Materials: Washable paints, brushes, shallow bowls or plates; blank paper (butcher-block paper works well); bubble wrap, old cardboard tubes, holiday cookie cutters, muffin tins (any size)

Why to do it: What is more charming than colorful wrapping paper, lovingly homemade? It also makes for a toddler craft that doesn't have to be saved, which has its advantages for those with increasingly limited storage and refrigerator display space.

How to do it: Printing is made for toddlers: It allows them to do the same thing, over and over. And the results are almost magical in their uniformity. These four easy homemade holiday prints can be used for wrapping Christmas, Hanukkah, or Kwanzaa gifts—just choose the colors to fit the holiday.

Holiday polka dots: Using washable tempera paints in holiday colors and a wide brush, flip over a muffin pan and let your toddler paint each of the circular bottoms that stick up. Now flip the pan over and press it down on your intended holiday paper. Presto: automatic polka dots!

Cookie-cutter shapes: Place a holiday cookie cutter on the paper you'll be using, and hold it in place with your hands. Now let your child paint the inside. You can put many such prints on the paper, or just a few. Whichever you choose, the results are sure to be appropriately cheery.

Rings: Cut a cardboard tube (like the kind inside wrapping paper, toilet paper, or paper towel rolls) into 3- to 4-inch segments. Pour a small amount of paint into shallow bowls or plates. Now let your child dip the open end of the tubes into the paint and then press

them on the paper for a colorful display of holiday rings.

Tiny bubbles: Save the bubble wrap that comes in your holiday packages and cut it into manageable 5- by 5-inch squares. Now let your child paint the tops of the bubbles with various colors of paint. When he's finished, lift the square and press it onto another piece of paper for a wild, snakeskin-like print.

MAKE ORNAMENTS

Suggested Ages: 18 months and up

Your Child's Special Skills and Interests: Painting, stringing beads, talking

Preparation Time: 15 minutes

Messiness Quotient: High—you're dealing with potentially loose glitter.

Materials: See below.

Commonsense Caution: Wash hands well, and remind kids to keep glittery fingers away from their face. Loose glitter can be painful in little eyes.

Why to try it: These activities are fun for your child, and result in what will surely be heirlooms for your tree.

How to do it: Prepare your work surface, then gather all the items you need for each of these crafts before beginning.

Snow Pinecones

Materials: Pinecones, white glue, paintbrush, glitter, plastic bag, dental floss

A child as young as a year and a half can make these shiny ornaments virtually from start to finish; even younger children may be able to do the shaking on of the glitter. To make one, put a large, open pinecone on a piece of paper and give your child a small paintbrush with a plate of white glue. Let her either roll the cone in the glue or paint the cone with it. Now put the pinecone in a plastic bag filled with several tablespoons of glitter and let her shake. Take out your now shiny pinecone, tap it on a piece of paper to release loose glitter, and let it dry. You can hang it on the tree with a piece of dental floss.

Beaded Snowflakes or Hanukkah Stars

Materials: White pipe cleaners, plastic beads, scissors, dental floss or fishing line

Once your child is old enough to string smallish beads, he can make these pretty little ornaments to hang in your windows or on your tree. You'll need white pipe cleaners and clear, white, or silver- or gold-colored beads with large enough holes to slip the pipe cleaners through. For a snowflake, cut the pipe cleaners in half, and pinch over one end of each. Now let your child string beads on each pipe cleaner half, securing it by pinching the other end of the pipe cleaner over. Lay the beaded

pipe cleaners across each other in a snowflake shape, securing them at the center with another piece of pipe cleaner. For a star, your child can bead two long pipe cleaners and then let you shape them into a Star of David, anchoring them with smaller pieces of pipe cleaner as necessary. Hang either ornament with a piece of clear dental floss or fishing line.

Memory Balls

Materials: Glass ball ornaments, permanent metallic markers

Everyone imagines hanging ornaments on the tree, year after year, and having them bring back happy memories. These glass balls will enhance your family's power of recall by giving you a written record of your memories. Using a metallic permanent paint marker, note the highlights of life in your family the last year on a blown-glass ball: trips, visitors, accomplishments. You can include the details of your child's life here, or

make a separate ball for him in addition to the family ball, so that he can put his own ball on his first tree. At first, of course, your child will have little to contribute to this process. But soon enough he'll be able to dictate what to add to the ball, and, even sooner, he'll be able to enjoy hearing what the balls "say" as they go on the tree.

MAKE GIFTS FOR GRANDPARENTS

Suggested Ages: 18 months and up

Your Child's Special Skills and Interests: Painting, drawing

Preparation Time: 10 minutes

Messiness Quotient: Medium to high

Materials: See below.

Why to try it: Teach your child about giving, endow art projects with new purpose, and help connect the generations by making gifts for grandparents and other friends and relatives.

How to do it: Let's face it, as gift-makers, your child's skills are pretty limited. But one thing they can do, starting about the age of 18 months or so, is paint and draw. To turn these early flashes of artistry into gifts, you simply have to provide the right things to paint and draw on.

Heirloom Dish Towel

Materials: Fabric paints, plain dish towels,
permanent markers, brushes

Turn plain white dish towel into treasured pieces of art, by letting your two-year-old paint or draw on them with fabric paints. (Because fabric paints are absolutely not washable, be sure to cover your work area well and dress your child appropriately.) To make these usually wildly colored dish towels even more personal, have your child tell you what it is that she's painted and write down what she says (if anything) with a permanent marker under each painting or drawing.

Rock the Refrigerator

Materials: Flat rocks, self-adhesive magnet strips,
washable tempera paints

Painting rocks to turn them into paperweights is an age-old craft, but for a more modern and possibly more practical twist, have your child paint small lightweight rocks and place self-adhesive magnets on the back of each stone to turn them

into kitchen magnets. If you choose flat rocks, these can easily be slipped in the mail, to adorn the refrigerators of your child's fans for many years to come.

Napkin Rings

Materials: Empty cardboard paper towel roll, decoupage glue, holiday paper napkins, ribbons, glitter

Turn a paper towel roll into a colorful set of holiday napkin rings in one short session. Limit your children's paint palette to holiday colors: shiny gold and silver and dark blue for Hanukkah; green, red, and black for Kwanzaa; or red and green for Christmas. Then let them paint away. Encourage them to

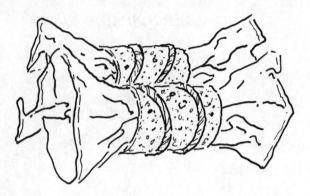

cover every bit of the gray of the paper towel roll, but make sure they don't soak the cardboard so thoroughly it collapses. Once they have finished and the paint is dry, you can cut it horizontally into 4- or 5-inch rings. At this point, your child can glue on extra decorations (ribbons, glitter) and then paint on a smooth, shiny, protective layer of decoupage glue, if you wish. Now stuff them each with a purchased paper holiday napkin, or simply box them up for giving. If you have the time and inclination to be even more elaborate, you can have your child paint matching holiday napkins on plain squares of fabric, with fabric paint.

MAKE A JINGLE-BELL BRACELET

Suggested Ages: 18 months and up, though younger babies will need adult supervision (so they won't work off a bell and eat it)

Your Child's Special Skills and Interests: Ringing in the holidays!

Preparation Time: 5 minutes

Messiness Quotient: Low

The Sibling Factor: Let the whole family ring away.

Materials: Scissors, elastic thread, jingle bells, blunt needle (the type used for plastic canvas works well)

Why to try it: It's a great way for baby to "ring" along with holiday music.

How to do it: You can make one of these jingle-bell bracelets yourself for a young child to wear (put it on a baby's foot and let her kick away) or let your toddler string one himself. Simply tie a large knot at one end so the bells won't slip off, then show your child how to thread a bunch of bells on the string. Make sure the bracelet (or anklet) is big enough so that it won't bite into your child's skin.

WRAP UP YOUR BLOCKS

Suggested Ages: Two years and up

Your Child's Special Skills and Interests: Taping, sticking, and ripping up paper

Preparation Time: 10 minutes

Messiness Quotient: Medium

The Sibling Factor: An older sibling might enjoy truly wrapping up blocks, even if just for practice for "real" wrapping.

Materials: Colored wooden building blocks, clear tape or colored masking tape, ribbon, wrapping paper, bows, holiday stickers

Why to try it: While you wrap your presents, let your child wrap his blocks. If you wish, you can turn this project into temporary ornaments for your tree by hanging them with fishing line from a branch, or set them on the table as a centerpiece.

How to do it: Lay out a half-dozen different-colored, rectangular blocks. Put out a number of small pieces of tape, stuck on the edge of the wall or table to be pulled up as needed. You'll also want square pieces of wrapping paper, scraps of ribbon, tiny bows, holiday stickers, and any other gift decorations you might have saved. Now, while you wrap your presents, let your child "wrap" his, taping on ribbon and paper, bows, and sticker tags. You can expect that some corners and sides of the blocks will still show, but since they are colored, assure your child that the gaps just add to the beauty of the gift. If you decide to use the blocks for decoration or ornaments, you can, of course, unwrap them and return them to the block box after the holidays.

MAKE A HOLIDAY COUNT-DOWN CALENDAR

Suggested Ages: Two years and up

Your Child's Special Skills and Interests: Understanding holidays are coming; needing help understanding when

Preparation Time: One hour for an adult to make alone

Messiness Quotient: Medium

The Sibling Factor: Naturally, you'll need enough treats for each child in the house stored in your treat bags.

Materials: New, holiday-themed dish cloth; wooden one-fourth-inch dowel cut to the width of the dish towel, metal-rimmed paper-circle key tags, plastic sandwich bags, 2 feet of colored ribbon; colored tissue paper, safety pins, hot-glue or staple gun; variety of age-appropriate bag-sized "treats"

Why to try it: This treat-a-day "advent" calendar will make each day of waiting for the holidays special, help your child

understand when—exactly—the holidays will arrive, and encourage her to develop concepts of time and practice counting. Plus, you can re-use it year after year, so it's worth the investment of time.

How to do it: Your final product will be a hanging fabric calendar, featuring numbered bags for each day of the month, each with a hidden treat inside. To make one:

1.   Glue or staple both ends of a strip of ribbon to the wooden dowel to create a hanger for the calendar.

2.   Glue or staple the dowel under the top edge of the dish towel.
3.   Loosely wrap all of your treats (stickers, candy, stick-on earrings, costume jewelry, tiny cars, plastic animals) in tissue paper and put them in the sandwich bags. Secure each bag closed with a ribbon and a numbered (for the day of the month) key tag.
4.   Safety-pin each treat bag onto your dishtowel in calendar order.
5.   Hang your calendar on the wall where treat bags can be removed once a day—right up until Christmas or Hanukkah. If you have an impatient soul in your home, you might hang it high enough to ensure that you are the one removing the bags: Safety pins will eventually poke persistent little fingers.

HAVE A WINTER HOLIDAY FOR THE BIRDS

Suggested Ages: Two years and up

Your Child's Special Skills and Interests: Sad to see the Christmas tree go

Preparation Time: 15 minutes

Messiness Quotient: High—peanut butter and loose seeds are involved.

The Sibling Factor: This can easily become a family tradition for all your family members, a perfect holiday transition activity between Christmas and the days when school resumes.

Materials: Sliced bread, peanut butter, wild bird food, paper clips; orange halves; dried cranberries, string, and blunt-tipped needle

Why to try it: Decorating the Christmas tree with edibles for the birds with bird cookies, orange cups, and cranberry rings is a great way to ease the sadness many children feel when the tree must be thrown out.

How to do it: Strip your Christmas tree of decorations and set it outside in its stand. Or choose a live evergreen or even a deciduous tree to decorate. Whatever your choice, it should be positioned where you'll be able to see and enjoy it from an indoor vantage point. Then make the following decorations.

 Bird Cookies. Let your child help you cut the crusts off the sliced bread if you wish (a table knife will work) and use holiday cookie cutters to cut it into festive shapes. Now heat the bread in a 300-degree oven until it is as dry as toast. Take it out of the oven, and let it cool. After you slather the bread with peanut butter, let your child either drop on the bird feed or press the bread into the bird feed. If you wish, you can decorate the bird cookies further with a few dried cranberries. Unbend half of a paper clip and stick one end through the bread, using the other as a hook to hang it on the tree.

 Orange Cups. If you juice your oranges, this is a great way to use the empty shells. For hangers, simply attach strings to the shells with half-open paper clips, and then let your child spoon bird seed into the shells and hang them on the tree.

 Cranberry Rings. String dried cranberries and O-shaped cereal on short strands as mini-wreaths. If you wish, you can use them to decorate your indoor tree first, then leave them intact when you move it outside. Using a blunt needle, help your child string the berries and cereal onto a 6-inch string (sometimes children like the job of pulling the cereal or cranberry down to the bottom of the string best). When

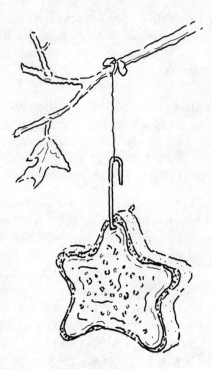

you reach the end, tie the two ends together to make a circular wreath you can hang on the tree. (Note: Although stringing popcorn garlands is a classic holiday decoration for indoor or outdoor trees, it requires a needle that is too sharp for your young child, and it is frustrating when the popcorn kernel breaks in half as you attempt to string it. As for using fresh cranberries, they are hard and likely to roll away while your child tries to skewer them. Besides, stringing an entire garland often requires too much patience.)

Kwanzaa

Kwanzaa is an African-American holiday based on seven guiding principles, the first of which is unity of family. To celebrate with your child under three, play up the elements of the holiday that are accessible for the very young, remembering that creativity is also one of its central themes.

MAKE A MKEKA

Materials: Approximately fifty pieces of wild grass, approximately 9 inches long; white glue, scissors and one piece white construction paper *or* two pieces black construction paper and two pieces each green and red construction paper, scissors and tape

A straw place mat called a Mkeka is the centerpiece of the Kwanzaa table. You can make one with your young child by letting him help you gather long pieces of grass that you can glue side-by-side onto a white piece of construction paper to give the appearance of a grass mat. You can also weave a Mkeka out of paper. Cut a half-dozen straight horizontal lines into a large piece (or two pieces taped together) of black construction paper. Now let your young child help you weave in and out alternating strips of green and red paper.

CREATE A KINARA

Materials: Wood; red, green, and black tempera paint; brushes, seven candles; optional: drill

The candleholder called a Kinara holds seven candles to reflect the seven principles of Kwanzaa. If you don't have one, think about ways in which your young child (even an 18-month-old) could help you make one. One possibility: Let your child paint a piece of wood with the Kwanzaa colors and then set seven candle votives atop the board. (If you have a drill, you could also drill holes for candles and their holders into the painted wood.)

Valentine's Day

Love is the primary lesson you teach your child every day. Valentine's Day gives you a chance to emphasize just how much you care and gives your child the opportunity to show love and friendship for others as well.

CREATE A FAMILY VALENTINE BOX

Materials: Red paper, shoebox, white glue, scissors

Cover a box with red paper and cut in a mail slot. Cut several dozen hearts out of red construction paper, and set them beside the box with a pen. In the weeks before Valentine's Day, write down things about your child (or children) that you love on the hearts and slip them in the box. Each

night at dinner or before bed, read a Valentine to each of your children. It won't be long before Valentine hearts begin to appear for you, even if your child has to dictate the messages to you in advance for you to write down or has to translate what she has written down herself for you to read.

DELIVER SOME LOVE AROUND TOWN

Materials: Red licorice strands, heart cookie cutter and sugar cookie ingredients, sandwich bags, or valentine stickers and heart candy

At the same time you show your children how much you love them, give them opportunities to feel the joy of giving love as well as receiving it. Pick a day around Valentine's Day when you'll be with your child all day. Make up a batch of heart-shaped sugar cookies—your child can stamp them out— then string them on strands of red licorice, one cookie per strand. Stick them in individual sandwich bags, and let your child hand out cookie necklaces to all his favorite friends: the waitress at your special lunch spot, the post office clerk, the grocery store checker, the friends he has at your office or at school. No time to bake? Have your child deliver Valentine stickers (he will love to stick these on his friends) or tiny bags of heart candy

WHAT TO DO DURING . . .

Easter and Spring

Celebrate the end of a long winter by getting out of the house. On your daily walks, search for shoots of green among the grass and leaves. Splurge on fresh flowers for your home. Eat strawberries. Go to the duck pond. Read stories about spring. Visit the local zoo to see the baby animals, or call a feed store to see if they have any young chicks.

And, on the first of May, revive the age-old May Day tradition of the May Basket in your neighborhood. Let your child help you fill a homemade basket with flowers (you can easily make a cone-shaped one out of a loosely rolled piece of construction paper). Just set it beside your neighbors' door or hang it on their doorknob and ring the doorbell, then hide out of sight so you can see their surprise. Children of all ages absolutely love this event—and your neighbors will too. In addition, try the following spring-holiday activities.

PLAY WITH PLASTIC EGGS

Suggested Ages: Nine months and up

Your Child's Special Skills and Interests: Rolling things, taking them apart, throwing

Preparation Time: 3 minutes

Messiness Quotient: Medium

Materials: Hollow plastic eggs of different sizes

Why to try it: Whether your children are unscrewing the eggs to open them or rolling them across the floor, simple plastic eggs provide inexpensive and easy fun around Easter.

How to do it:

Serve an egg meal. Starting when she is about nine months or a year of age, surprise your child by placing three or four plastic eggs on her high-chair tray at snack or meal time. Let her shake the eggs and roll them, then (as necessary) show her what is inside: dried cereal in one, tiny crackers in another, and so forth.

Have an egg roll. Get down on your hands and knees with your crawling or toddling child and put an egg in front of you on a slick, hard floor. Now, start rolling the egg across the room. Because eggs roll unevenly, young kids find this activity challenging but hilarious. If you have older siblings, handicap them in this race (and yourself as well) by requiring that they push the egg with their nose.

Try an egg toss. Play a game of catch with a large, empty plastic egg with your two-and-a-half- or three-year-old. The egg is lightweight and fairly easy to catch, as long as the distance is quite small between you. If tossing doesn't work, just roll the egg back and forth.

Have your own personal-sized Easter egg hunt. Children under three don't usually compete well with older kids in a traditional egg hunt. Most have never had things truly hidden from them, and they also lack the necessary competitive instinct. So have your own, small-scale, hidden-in-plain-view Easter egg hunt. And don't confine yourself to hunts just on Easter morning: You can have several egg hunts before the actual holiday. In fact, if your child will be going to a bigger hunt on Easter, these could be helpful as trial runs.

GROW YOUR OWN EASTER BASKET

Suggested Ages: 18 months and up

Your Child's Special Skills and Interests: Playing in dirt

Preparation Time: 10 minutes

Messiness Quotient: High—loose dirt is involved.

Materials: Wicker basket, aluminum foil, plastic wrap, potting mix, grass seed, food coloring, brushes

Why to try it: The plastic grass you usually put in baskets is a mess, especially in the hands of a two-year-old. A live Easter basket is a pretty change, and offers an easy beginning gardening project.

How to do it: Line a tightly woven wicker basket with foil and plastic and then let your child help you scoop potting soil inside with a plastic measuring cup (put down towels or paper to protect the mess if you have to do this in the house). Now let your child help you sprinkle fast-growing grass seed on top of the soil. Set it in a sunny place two weeks before Easter, and give your child the job of watering it lightly daily. If you have a green thumb, you and your child may even need to give your basket a "hair cut" (with child-safe scissors) before Easter if the grass gets too long. After Easter, if you live in a climate where your own lawn has started to grow, you might even be able to transplant the basket-grown grass into the yard.

Advanced Variation: Before you begin growing your Easter basket, let your child paint it with food coloring (put a few drops of each color in mill jug lids). As long as the wicker of the basket isn't varnished, in which case it might not take the paint, the dye will soak into the basket material to create a soft, pastel, mottled look.

MAKE AN INCREDIBLE, NON-EDIBLE, EGG

Suggested Ages: 18 months and up

Your Child's Special Skills and Interests: Playing with squishy stuff

Preparation Time: 30 minutes

Messiness Quotient: High

The Sibling Factor: Let an older sibling participate in the preparation of the mixture the night before. Because the reaction between the ingredients takes place so rapidly, making this substance is a special kick for older kids.

Materials: White glue, Borax, food coloring, container with lid,
bowl, measuring cups

Why to try it: As an alternative to Easter-induced sugar over-load.

How to do it: Make up a batch of this elastic-like substance that is stretchy and gooey—but not sticky, except in contact with cloth—and use it to fill a few of your child's plastic eggs this Easter.

To make it:

1. Mix half a cup of Borax with two cups of water in a con-tainer with a lid.
2. Shake thoroughly, and keep shaking. Don't let the Borax settle.
3. Mix a cup of glue with a cup of water in another jar and stir well.
4. Now put three tablespoons of the well-shaken Borax mix-ture in a bowl. Add three-eighths of a cup of the glue water and whatever color you prefer. With just a few stirs (the more you stir the firmer it gets) it will begin to solidify into a weird kind of slimy putty. Play with it outside or in the kitchen: It becomes sticky as soon as it comes into contact with carpeting or other fabrics. Roll the putty into balls and then watch as they "melt" back into goo, or imprint it with cookie cutters and watch the shapes disappear. And the stuff bounces too! Fill plastic eggs with it and place them in the basket. Your kids will be so excited about them, they might almost forget about eating their entire chocolate bunny.

Jokester's Variation: If you are feeling particularly silly, color a small batch of the putty with bright yellow food col-oring.

Stick the yellow putty in the center of the white putty to create for a nearly perfect imitation of hard-boiled eggs.

WHAT TO DO DURING . . .

THE SUMMER HOLIDAYS

Who cares that Memorial Day and Labor Day are such holiday duds (aside from the fireworks, of course)? The whole summer is full of holiday-like possibilities, most of which have to do with water, from paddling about in pools to wading (with sandals) in creeks to running through sprinklers. And that's just the beginning. In case you've forgotten, here is a list of the traditional summer events of childhood, scaled down to suit even a baby's abilities and interests. Another reminder from childhood: Watch out for hot seats, hot cement, stinging bugs, and burning sun. Summer isn't *all* bliss. Just mostly.

- Splash in shallow puddles. Strip your child down and let her pound her hands and feet (if she's walking) in the water you've let pool from the hose in the shade on the driveway. If the cement isn't too hot, she can make prints with her hands and feet and watch them evaporate.

- Sit by moving water and throw in sticks. With your child securely in your control, find a river, a creek, a culvert—even water running down the driveway or the gutter—and throw in sticks or pieces of grass, then watch them float by. This is endlessly, ridiculously amusing.

● Make a splash. Find a pond, a wading pool—even use a bucket, if that's all you've got handy. Let your child drop in the heaviest objects she can safely handle and then stand back and watch as she screams with delight.

● Have a water-balloon roll. Fill a water balloon three-fourths full with ice-cold water—not completely full, because you don't want the balloon to break. Roll the balloon back and forth to your baby or toddler. Just touching the balloon and squishing it between his hands will delight your child. If it breaks, pick up all the pieces immediately: *Latex balloons are a serious choking hazard.*

WHAT TO DO DURING . . .

HALLOWEEN AND AUTUMN

For obvious reasons, many parents don't want to introduce their child to the ghoulish side of Halloween. But there remains much about this holiday with real little-kid appeal: painting on yourself, dressing up, and pumpkins, just to name a few.

You can also use the days before and after Halloween to celebrate autumn. The fall leaves will often just be reaching their peak around now. Almost any toddler can help you rake (especially if provided with his own downsized version of the tool), and as soon as they can walk, young children are only too happy to kick and jump in and throw the downed fall foliage. And be sure to take advantage of the fall harvest, if there is such a thing in your area. Call your local chamber of commerce to determine if there are any pick-it-yourself farms in your area, then head to one, equipped with a portable stepping stool to help your shortest family member reach the ripest fruit or vegetable.

PAINT YOUR PUMPKINS

Suggested Ages: 18 months and up

Your Child's Special Skills and Interests: Painting

Preparation Time: 5 minutes

Messiness Quotient: Medium

Materials: Paintbrushes, washable tempera paints,
a pumpkin or two

Why to try it: Young kids can't draw pumpkin faces or cut jack-o-lanterns. Which is why this simple but fun Halloween craft is just your toddler's speed.

How to do it: Prepare and protect your work area, set out a pumpkin and paints, and then let your child get started. Turn the pumpkin around at regular intervals so your child will be able to paint the whole thing. When he's finished, you can use the wild-colored squash as a unique centerpiece for a few days, then cut it into a jack-o-lantern and set it outside.

LET YOUR CHILD MAKE HIS COSTUME

Suggested Ages: 18 months and up

Your Child's Special Skills and Interests: Dressing up, painting

Preparation Time: 30 minutes

Messiness Quotient: High

The Sibling Factor: If your child has older siblings,
they may insist that their younger sibling be
something recognizable.

Materials: Sweats, fabric paints and brushes, scarves, plain
headbands, jewelry, face paints, scissors, pillowcases,
hot-glue gun

Why to try it: Why not let your child show you his creativity and imagination this Halloween by allowing him to make his own costume (with your help, of course)? His costume may

not be as fancy and clever as the store-bought version, but he can take real pride in what he's wearing.

How to do it: Provide your child with a basic "canvas" for his costume. You can buy plain-colored sweats (the basis of a warm costume) or cut arm and head holes out of an old plain pillowcase. Besides this foundation, set out other items for possible use and inspiration: feathers, costume jewelry, felt scraps, scarves, and so forth. Simply looking at all this material may inspire your child to be a horse or a pig, or he may need suggestions from you to help him make up his mind. Once you've determined, what—if any specific thing—your child intends to dress up as, get started making his costume with him. Your

child can paint his own designs on his sweats or tell you where to glue or stick various items. Some ideas to get you thinking:

Painter: If your child already loves to paint, let him dress as an artist in painted clothes and with a painted face and carrying a cardboard palette and brush in his hand. Draw on a Parisian moustache and buy a beret to complete the look.

Pig: Dress your child in pink sweats, which she can cover with paint marks to look like mud; paint her face; and glue or staple on a squiggly tail made out of a pipe cleaner. Cardboard ears can be attached to a plain-colored headband.

Native American: Let him paint his own tribal marks on his pillowcase smock, into which you've cut fringes at the bottom. Face paint and a headband full of feathers should complete the look.

GIVE OUT THE GHOSTS

Suggested Ages: Two years and up

Your Child's Special Skills and Interests: Giving out treats to callers or friends

Preparation Time: 5 minutes

Messiness Quotient: Low

The Sibling Factor: These treats are easier for older children to make and younger kids to play with and give out.

Materials: Round-ball-type lollipops, white tissue or squares of white sheet, twist ties, black marker, floral foam

Why to try it: These treats are fun to make, give out—and have puppet shows with.

How to do it: Simply drape the lollipops with a square of tissue or cloth and secure them below the candy with a twist tie. Then draw faces on the tissue or cloth with a black marker. Stick your "ghosts" together in a hunk of floral foam and let them haunt your door until trick-or-treaters begin to arrive. Then let your toddler help you give out the ghosts.

WHAT TO DO FOR . . .

YOUR BABY'S BIRTHDAYS

The First Birthday

Of course, baby's first birthday is about you. Your child is too young to really appreciate the celebration being held in his behalf. But that's okay. There is much worth celebrating. Primarily, of course, the first birthday is an important benchmark of your life as a parent. You've survived sleepless nights, afternoon crying fits, first teeth, and first fevers. So go ahead and have a party. And since you are celebrating survival, be sure to invite the people who helped you realize it: your friends, your family, and your child's babysitters, of course. Any young friends your child may have should also be welcome, too, especially if they are old enough to help open baby's gifts (he probably won't be interested in doing this for any length of time); and wearing their own party hats, they can increase the mood of reverie.

Plan this first celebration for a time during the day when your baby is relatively certain to be at his most awake and alert, since you'll certainly want him in attendance. You might also want to think about any birthday traditions you'd like to begin now, as well as any records you'd like to have for your baby's scrapbook or memory box. One easy tradition that helps you date every photograph for years to come: Use fabric paint to write your child's age in a large single numeral on a plain T-shirt or sweat shirt for him to wear. This special birthday outfit will also get attention from others, of course, giving your child a chance to tell others exactly how old he is. In years to come, he'll even be able to make his own shirt.

If you have most of your closest and dearest friends and relations present, you might also try to get single photographs of each person at this first birthday party, either to turn into kitchen magnets (see Chapter 3, "Nap Times") or to use to create baby's scrapbook of friends. For party favors for your guests, give them a photo kitchen magnet of their favorite little guy: your baby.

The Second Birthday

If your child has been to many other birthday parties, she may have some idea of what awaits her. Still, much of her own birthday celebration will be surprising and potentially overwhelming. Make a guest list that takes into account your child's capacity to deal with crowds and her current level of stranger anxiety. In other words, you'll probably want to keep the party small and short, and scheduled for her happiest time of day. If your child is going through a possessive "mine" stage, or you suspect that other guests are going through it, you might keep the gift-opening low-key. Instead of the usual group event with a bunch of kids lusting after the gift they just gave to the guest of honor, consider letting your child open the gifts immediately as they are presented to her when the guests arrive, or possibly after they've left.

Keep activities easy and simple, and, if you can, make party favors double as a party event. Two easy activities for either the second or third birthday party include the following.

Make Paper Party Hats:

1. Set out white paper bakery bags (about lunch-bag size), allowing one for each guest. Open each bag and roll up the bottom to make a "brim."

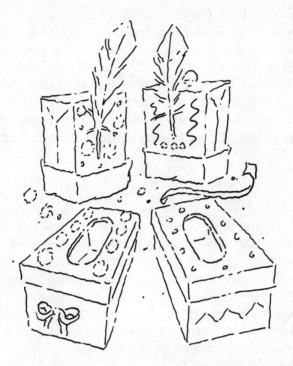

2. Cover the work surface, and set out bowls of decorative gluables—scraps of ribbon, feathers, pom poms, and so forth. Give each partygoer either a glue stick or a small pool of white glue in a tiny paper cup and an ear swab to apply paint with, then let the children attach the decorations to their hats. If you'd like, you can also let partygoers paint their hats with washable paints, although this does involve a higher level of potential mess.

Make Special Party Shoes:

Your partygoers can keep on painting and gluing: These special square shoes are a blast for kids to try to make and wear. Just follow these steps:

1. Stockpile kid-size shoeboxes until you have enough to pro-
    vide a set of two for each guest. Tape the lid securely onto
    every box before your guests arrive, and cut a foot-size hole
    in the top.
2. Set a pair of boxes in front of each guest, and let them paint
    or glue things onto them to decorate their "shoes."
3. While the shoes (and hats) dry, eat the birthday cake.
4. Get a group picture of everyone in their party best!

The Third Birthday

Your child almost certainly knows about his birthday by this
third year, and while he may have no real expectations for a
party, why not throw one anyway? If you keep the guest list
small and the activities manageable, this will be a party your
child will remember for months to come, even if he may not
recall it in the long run. Just as with the party at two years of
age, you might keep the emphasis on gift opening low-key:
Nothing could be worse to many three-year-olds than watching somebody else get a gift. For your party events this year
consider the following:

Hunt for peanuts: Spray-paint a bunch of unshelled peanuts various colors, and hide them around the house.
Having them work in teams (with a reader and counter
in each), send the children out to look for a certain
number of peanuts of each color.

Crown your guests: Before your guests arrive, cut a crown
for each of them out of a double-layer of felt. Stick on
a Velcro strip at each end for the closure. When the
guests arrive, let them decorate their crowns with glitter glue and paste-on "jewels," available at craft stores.

Let them all eat cake: In addition to the birthday cake,
make cupcakes for the partygoers and frost them before

your guests arrive. Now set out cups of candies, sprinkles, and squeeze-on frostings on a covered table. While the guest of honor decorates his own birthday cake, let her guests decorate their cupcakes. This activity creates a mess, but it's extremely popular.